The Bushmen
of Southern Africa

The Bushmen
of Southern Africa

*A Foraging Society
in Transition*

Andy Smith, Candy Malherbe,
Mat Guenther & Penny Berens

DAVID PHILIP PUBLISHERS Cape Town
OHIO UNIVERSITY PRESS Athens

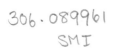
First published 2000 in southern Africa by David Philip Publishers (Pty) Ltd,
208 Werdmuller Centre, Claremont 7708;
and in North America by Ohio University Press,
Scott Quadrangle, Athens, Ohio 45701, United States of America

ISBN 0-86486-419-1 (David Philip)
ISBN 0-8214-1341-4 (Ohio University Press)

Library of Congress Cataloging-in-Publication Data
available upon request from the publisher

Text design by Abdul Amien
Layout by Gretel Eastwood
Cover by Abdul Amien

Reproduction by Fairstep, Cape Town, South Africa
Printed by Clyson Printers, Maitland, Cape Town, South Africa

Contents

Acknowledgements

We would like to thank our colleagues who have so freely shared their knowledge: Megan Biesele, Rein Dekker, Bob Hitchcock, Susan Kent, Richard Lee, Braam & Willemien le Roux, John Parkington, Karim Sadr, Judy Sealy, Axel Thoma and Polly Wiessner. We are also grateful to the many Bushman friends who have worked with us to share their own life and history, particularly those people from D'Kar Village in Botswana and in the Nyae Nyae area of Namibia. We hope this book gives them strength in their cause to claim important space for their children.

Note on pronunciation

Clicks used in Bushman languages

All Khoesaan languages have clicks, which are additional consonants. If the click is missing the word is incomplete, just as if a letter were omitted from a word in English. The most commonly used clicks are:

/   Dental click, made by placing the tongue behind the front teeth to make the sound 'tut'.

≠   Alveolar click, made by sucking the tongue against the ridge behind the upper front teeth.

//   Lateral click, made at the side of the mouth.

!   Palatal click, made by clucking the tongue on the roof of the palate.

CHAPTER ONE

An introduction to the hunting people

Much has been written about the Bushmen of Africa – their distant past, their recent past and their present way of life. This book brings together evidence of their pre-colonial history and their interface with farming people. It documents the events which overtook them when they came into contact with expanding European interests and attempts to describe a traditional culture which had adapted to many different environments but which ultimately survived only in the most remote areas of southern Africa. Archaeology, history and social anthropology show that the Bushmen did not just disappear but strongly resisted the takeover of their land, although at a high cost in lives. Many of the surviving Bushmen became virtual slaves to farmers in the interior and subsequently became part of the 'coloured' community.

New forces are at work on groups which still live in Botswana and Namibia, where formerly marginal lands have now been opened up for farming by the drilling of new boreholes. This has further marginalised hunting populations, who see their territories being eroded. Their response has been to forge new identities and links with threatened aboriginal people worldwide.

This book is an introduction to the hunter-foragers of southern Africa and describes their lifestyle as it developed into a sophisticated means of extracting a livelihood within the different types of environment at the southern end of the African

1.1: *Ju/'hoansi Bushmen from Nyae Nyae pans, Namibia, leaving for a hunting and foraging trip.*

1 • The use of names (San, Bushmen, Khoekhoen, Khoesaan) •

Some confusion exists in the use of names. The hunters today have no collective name for themselves. They use their own group names, such as Ju/'hoansi (people who live on the border between northern Namibia and Botswana), or Hai//om (people who live around Etosha National Park).

San = Sonqua = Soaqua was a name given to hunters by the Khoekhoen of the Cape. The word means 'people different from ourselves' and became associated with those without stock, or people who stole stock. The names are thus generally negative and refer to 'the other' or 'them'. In 1668 the European writer Dapper described the Sonquas as people who 'have no cattle, but live by shooting rockrabbits [and] ... big game'. They ate 'certain roots growing in the ground'. Dapper continues: 'They are extremely great plunderers and marauders. They steal from other Hottentots [as the Dutch called the herders] all the cattle they can get ... Their huts [are] made only of branches twined together ... and covered with rushes ... they never break up the huts, but erect still others wherever they camp.'

The name 'Bushman' or 'Bossiesman' was given to low-status people encountered by the Dutch settlers in the 1600s, and referred to those who collected their food off the land and had no domestic animals. Today, while the hunters have no single name for themselves, they have come to prefer outsiders using the term 'Bushman'.

Khoekhoen = Khoikhoi = Kwena is a general name which the herding people of the Cape (Boonzaier et al. 1996) used for themselves. To choose the use of the spelling 'Khoekhoen' (non-gender specific 'people' plural) is to follow Nama first-language speakers in Namibia today, and the way they write their language; Khoekhoe or Khoe (without the 'n' suffix) will be used as an adjective. The word can be translated to mean 'the real people' or 'men of men', meaning 'we people with domestic animals' as opposed to the Sonqua or Bushmen who had none, who often worked for the Khoekhoen, and were seen as lower class. As the diary of Simon van der Stel's trip to Namaqualand in 1685 describes: 'these Sonquas are just the same as the poor in Europe, each tribe of Hottentots having some of them and employing them to bring news of the approach of a strange tribe. They steal nothing from the kraals of their employers, but regularly from other kraals ... possessing nothing ... except what they acquire by theft.'

Khoesaan = Khoisan is a general term which linguists use for the click languages of southern Africa, and which physical anthropologists use as a biological term to distinguish the aboriginal people of southern Africa from their black African farming neighbours. The name may also be applied to those groups who are culturally difficult to distinguish, such as refugees of both Khoekhoen and Bushmen who were compelled to live together when the expanding Dutch colony forced many people off their land in the 1600s and 1700s.

The real confusion arises when racial terms are mixed with culture and language, as there are often no clear boundaries between the categories. For example, there are Khoe-speaking Bushmen living in northern Namibia.

continent. It is concerned with the impact that farming people have had on the hunters, as domestic animals and crops gradually expanded into most of southern Africa and compares the way of life of hunters with that of farmers and herders, examining the complexities of social relations between the groups.

Beginning in the 1400s, Europeans began

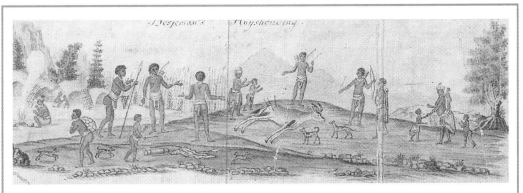

1.2: *Part of map showing a Bushman settlement in the northern Cape, by Col. Robert Gordon (undated, but probably drawn around 1785). Gordon was commander of the Dutch garrison at the Cape until the first British occupation in 1795. He made several long journeys into the interior, where he came in contact with Khoesaan people.*

exploring the world's oceans. When they reached the Americas, southern Africa, the islands of the Far East and Australia they found that many of the people they met lived off the land without any domesticated animals or plants. Such people we refer to as hunter-gatherers or foragers. Within foraging communities there is a sexual divison of labour with, in almost all cases, men hunting game animals, and women collecting wild plant foods.

Because they rely so heavily on the local available foods they know the different seasons for plant collecting, as well as the behaviour of the animals they hunt, so much of their lifestyle revolves around strategies to exploit these resources efficiently. Their life is often one of movement of camps between patches of food and water on a seasonal basis. Until around 12 000 years ago the entire world was occupied by foraging people. It was only after this date that humans learned to domesticate plants and animals in various parts of the world, with the result that farming communities began to spread into areas with good

soils and plenty of water.

The lifestyle of a number of surviving hunting groups has changed dramatically over the past thirty years as the modern world has encroached upon their territories. In the process the hunters have adopted new ways of living which have had to be incorporated into their existing social and cultural frameworks. These changes offer information about the process hunters undergo to become food producers themselves.

The three disciplines involved in this book are archaeology (Andy Smith), history (Candy Malherbe) and social anthropology (Mat Guenther). We use different kinds of information in our respective fields, and the way we apply our individual methods to gain our data will be explained in the text. By combining these three disciplines the amount of information available offers a wide range of ideas and debate about people whose culture has changed radically over the past decades, and, within a very short period of time, may not be available as the older generations disappear.

CHAPTER TWO

The Stone Age archaeology of southern Africa

What is archaeology?

Historians use the written word to understand and interpret the past, but for earlier times – 'prehistory' – archaeologists have to rely upon 'material culture', the things people left behind, to study the way these early people lived.

Let us create an archaeological site in our minds. We are at a picnic with friends. We cook meat on an open fire, and as soon as it is ready we get our plates and pile them up with meat and vegetables, and sit down with a cold drink. If we are not too fussy about keeping the area clean we just drop our bones on the ground, along with the empty drink can. Once we go away, we leave behind cans and bones and other bits and pieces. An archaeologist wanting to re-create what happened at this site would make a map of the whole area where there were signs of activity, marking and listing every item. All the material she or he could find would be collected, and each piece marked so the archaeologist could reconstruct exactly where it came from and its relationship to the others. The pieces would then be sorted into their different categories. Food would be one, including bones and pieces of vegetable; drinking containers another, for both alcoholic and non-alcoholic drinks. Looking at these items and their distribution, the archaeologist would derive a rough notion of how many people were at the picnic, what they ate, and where certain tasks, such as cooking, were performed.

This is exactly what happens on an archaeological site, except the archaeologists usually have to dig down into the earth to find the items from the past. If the debris from our picnic was left long enough it would eventually be covered over, and

should a second picnic take place, the remains from this new event would lie on top of the first. On excavating both, archaeologists would know that the older picnic was on the bottom, and the younger on top. This estimation of age is called 'relative dating'. Assuming the second event took place long after the first, the items, like drink cans, might be of different design or made of different metal. It would now be possible to consider changes in the material culture.

Ideas about culture change and the way items of material culture were used are basic to archaeological interpretation. From our restricted view of one site we can expand our vision of the particular society by excavating many sites. The more information we have the more accurate our knowledge of how people lived. We would like to expand this into uncovering what the people in the past thought and believed.

Of course, people are not just passive actors on a blank landscape. The resources of the countryside influence where and when they will do things. Equally, people will eventually change the landscape through their activities, such as farming or building settlements. Even hunters burning the veld to chase game will, over time, change the vegetation of an area.

Africa – the ultimate homeland

One of the questions many people ask is: where did the Bushmen come from? To answer this question is, in many ways, to find out where we all come from, since Africa is the ultimate homeland of the ancestors of us all.

Early humans, defined on the basis of having small canine teeth and walking on two feet, first developed on the African continent around 5 million years ago. We share ancestry with modern chimpanzees. Evidence from our body chemistry (DNA and proteins) shows that we are 97,6 per cent similar to chimpanzees, about the same as horses are to zebras. While one branch of the early human family was adapted to living in a woodland environment and so could take refuge in trees, another branch was forced to spend more time living on the ground.

Changes in climate and the effect on early humans

Around 5 million years ago there was a major climatic change which dramatically affected tropical Africa. This was a cooling event and it meant the disappearance of large areas of forest; open grassland started to appear.

2.1: *Evolution of humans from ape ancestry.*

2 • Littlefoot •

A recent piece of palaeontological detective work by Ron Clarke and his co-workers has led to a rethinking of how fully bipedal our early ancestors were. Clarke was able to match up two foot bones from Sterkfontein dated to over 3 million years ago. On the basis of these bones, one of which was a big toe bone, he suggested that the big toe was at an angle to the other toes, and so possibly opposable: thus it could be used to grasp things, as chimpanzees do today. This would mean that at this stage our ancestors may still have been efficient tree-climbers, even though they walked on two legs. Having matched the bones in the laboratory, Clarke asked his assistants, Kwane Molefe and Stephen Motsumi, to take a cast of the foot bones and see if they could match them up with other bones still in the rock walls of the cave.

At Sterkfontein, fossilised bones are embedded in a rock formation which has become solid, like concrete, and can only be 'excavated' by using a rock chisel or a pneumatic drill or be loosened by dynamite. Taking hand lamps down into the dark cav-

ern, Molefe and Motsumi scanned the rock walls, and with incredible skill and good fortune saw and recognised one small piece of bone in the wall which fitted on to the cast they held in their hands. Subsequent excavation by the team showed that most of the skeleton still remains in place, including the entire skull. Once it is fully excavated, this should prove to be the most complete australopithecine skeleton found so far.

But not everyone accepts Clarke's reconstruction of the big toe bones as being separate from the other toes. An American researcher, Bruce Latimer, argues that Clarke has exaggerated the separation of the toes – the creature was more like ourselves, and the foot bones were all in line. Such a pattern can be seen in the famous footprints from Laetoli in Tanzania, found by Mary Leakey and dated to 3,8 million years ago, which show two individuals with their toes all in line walking across freshly spewed volcanic dust, which hardened after the rains, preserving the footprints for all time.

Creatures living in the forest had to adapt to these changes. While there was still room for some earlier forms of chimpanzees in the diminishing forest, other groups had to make do in more open environments. This made them very vulnerable to attack by large carnivores, such as sabre-tooth lions or hyenas.

Those who were best able to see a potential threat by standing on their hind legs survived, and are known to scientists as *Australopithecus* (southern ape). By 4 million years ago our ancestors were fully bipedal (walking on two legs), and the big toe had become in line with the other toes for more efficient walking. This was different from the chimpanzee descendants who still had an opposable toe for climbing trees.

Walking on two legs meant that these ground-adapted early people moved more slowly than four-legged creatures. Our ancestors would have been dependent on their social group and on tools for defence.

It is not until around 2,5 million years ago that we start to recognise some of these tools at archae-

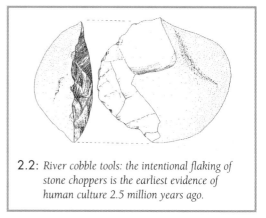

2.2: *River cobble tools: the intentional flaking of stone choppers is the earliest evidence of human culture 2.5 million years ago.*

ological sites, because this was when stone was first intentionally shaped. Stone, of course, survived where the wooden tools used previously have disappeared. The first stone tools were simple river cobbles bashed together to knock off flakes, giving a sharp cutting edge. We can recognise these as intentional tools because they are often found with the broken bones of large animals, and the source of the stone can be as much as three

3 • The Stone Age •

In 1800 an Englishman named John Frere published a description of an excavation done in Suffolk, where he recognised that stone tools found at a depth of over 50 centimetres were 'evidently weapons of war, fabricated and used by a people who had not the use of metals'.

The importance of this discovery was not really widely understood until 1836 when J.C. Boucher de Perthes, a Frenchman, described stone tools he had found in association with extinct fossil animal bones, pre-dating the biblical Flood, thus proving that humans once lived in a time very different from the present.

The term 'Stone Age' was first coined in the same year, 1836, when the Danish archaeologist Christian Jurgensen Thomsen, in his guidebook to the Copenhagen Museum, described his famous 'three-age system' – Stone Age, Bronze Age and Iron Age – and

organised the museum's antiquities according to this chronological scheme.

Stone Age refers to a time before the smelting of metals was invented, when the most durable implements in a culture were made of stone. Although natural stone pieces with sharp edges could be used as tools, humans learned to control the flaking of stone, especially of fine-grained rocks, like flint or chert. By controlling the type of flakes which were knocked off a core, the flint-knapper was able to shape them into different tool forms, to be used for cutting, drilling or scraping.

As human skills at flaking developed, there was an increase in the tool types through time. Stone tools became increasingly smaller (some only a centimetre in size) as people developed compound tools, such as pieces of stone embedded in wood or bone hafts to make spears, arrows and knives.

kilometres away. These tools belonged to the earliest part of the Early Stone Age of Africa.

Early humans

Humans are part of the zoological order Primates, which includes apes (chimpanzees, gorillas, orang utans), monkeys (baboons, vervets) and prosimians (pre-monkeys such as lemurs and bushbabies). The family of humans is called Hominidae. In Hominidae there are two groups: the extinct *Australopithecus*, and *Homo*.

We therefore refer to our ancestors as 'early hominids'. The first of the early hominids was found in the limeworks at Taung in the Northern Cape and identified by Raymond Dart in 1924. He named it *Australopithecus*, which means 'southern ape'. We now know that this specimen is about 3 million years old.

The earliest creature which is sufficiently like ourselves to be called *Homo* lived in East Africa around 2,5 million years ago, and is called *Homo habilis* (handy man), because this is also when we see the first stone tools appearing.

The first hominid to move outside Africa to the Middle East and Europe, and as far as China and Indonesia 800 000 years ago, is called *Homo erectus* (upright human). Early people whom we can refer to as archaic *Homo sapiens* (wise human) appeared in Africa around 200 000 years ago.

Anatomically modern people developed in two directions about 100 000 years ago. One branch

2.3: *Raymond Dart and the Taung juvenile skull, dated to before 3 million years ago.*

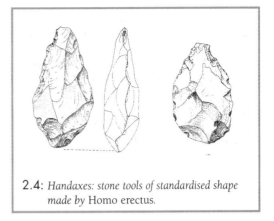

2.4: *Handaxes: stone tools of standardised shape made by* Homo erectus.

was the Neanderthals (*Homo sapiens neanderthalensis*), who ultimately became extinct, and the other *Homo sapiens sapiens*, our own species.

Early humans: hunters or scavengers?

The next development in the Early Stone Age is the appearance of handaxes. These tools were made by *Homo erectus*, who first appeared in Africa some 1,5 million years ago, and had a greater mental ability than his ancestors. The toolmakers could see the finished tool in their minds before they started flaking the stone, and were able to communicate so successfully that the handaxe became a standard tool form that was repeated over and over again throughout Africa, the Middle East and Europe.

The earliest stone tools have been discovered in Kenya, Tanzania and Ethiopia in East Africa. They are often found with the smashed bones of large animals. At first archaeologists assumed that hominids had hunted these animals, but a careful examination of the parts of the body from which the bones came showed they were mostly leg bones and other non-meaty parts of the animals. This probably means the hominids were getting only the left-overs from the meals of other animals, and so had access only to those parts of the body that remained after other animals had finished with the more meaty sections. What remained for the hominids was the marrow in the leg bones, which even the powerful jaws of hyenas could not crunch, but which the early humans could smash with their stone tools. We can thus assume that at this stage of human development people were scavenging meat from the kills of more effective hunters, such as lions.

The earliest evidence we have for tools that could have been used to hunt big game (or animals bigger than humans themselves) is 2-metre-long spears from Germany. These have been found along with many bones of wild horses that were the preferred food of the hunters at that time and are dated to around 300 000 years ago. By this time increasing brain size and maturing mental ability can be inferred from the more sophisticated stone tool-making.

4 • Bushman bow and arrow •

The hunting equipment of Bushmen relies heavily on poison to immobilise the prey. The result is that the bow does not need to be very powerful, but the hunter must get close to the animal, which requires skilful stalking. The poisonous arrow just needs to penetrate the skin, rather than to shock the system, as would occur with more powerful bows. The arrow is made up of three parts.

- The head, made of bone or wood with a stone (later metal) tip. The poison was applied immediately below the tip. This way a person or child could cut themselves but not be poisoned.
- The head was fixed into a link shaft, a piece of bone or wood that separated the head from the main reed shaft.
- The main reed shaft, which had feathers on the end to control the flight of the arrow.

If the beast ran through thick bush when the arrow hit it, instead of the whole arrow being knocked off by the bushes only the arrow shaft would be dislodged. The arrowhead was thus left attached to the animal, allowing the poison time to work through the body. The shaft could be picked up by the hunter and re-used.

Drawings of Bushmen made in the 1800s show spare arrow points shoved into the head band worn by hunters so their arrows could be quickly 're-loaded'.

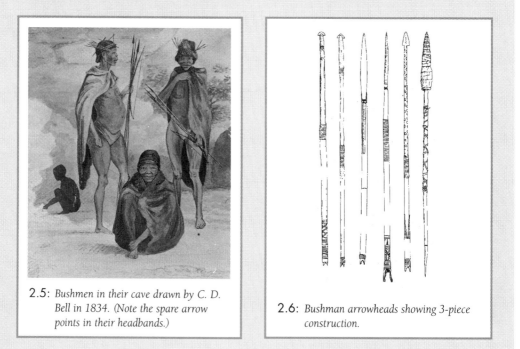

2.5: *Bushmen in their cave drawn by C. D. Bell in 1834. (Note the spare arrow points in their headbands.)*

2.6: *Bushman arrowheads showing 3-piece construction.*

The next innovation was a flaking technique called the 'prepared core', also known as the Levallois technique, after the place in France where it was first recognised. The advantage of this technique to the skilful flint-knapper was that by carefully preparing the core (the stone from which the flakes would be removed), sharp triangular points could be produced. It was at this period perhaps that the first compound hafted spears appeared, by means of which the sharp points were attached to a wooden shaft.

One of the risks of big-game hunting was that it was dangerous to get close enough to game animals to kill them. Those animals that might have been hunted up to this time would all have been smaller than the early hunters. By using a spear that could be thrown there was less danger of the hunter becoming the hunted. One can say that the intentional hunting of big-game animals (rather than scavenging) may well stem from the invention of the spear.

These spear-makers were early *Homo sapiens*, and their inventions show how innovative people were becoming. This period is referred to by archaeologists working in Africa as the Middle Stone Age. We find many cave sites occupied by people at this time throughout southern Africa.

Different stone-tool flaking techniques continued to be experimented with during this period. This is probably an indication of experimentation in other areas as well, such as the development of the social group which we call 'the family' today.

Archaeologists Chris Henshilwood and Judy Sealy have shown that at Blombos, near the southern tip of Africa, ochre and polished bone tools were being used between 50 000 and 60 000 years ago. Some 20 000 years ago there was a general resurgence of tool-making, involving small tools, which is referred to as the Later Stone Age. This is the time when people like ourselves who, in southern Africa, may be considered the direct ancestors of the Bushmen were to be found in different environments throughout the subcontinent.

The small tools of the Later Stone Age (called microliths) were used as arrowheads and as the blades of cutting tools for harvesting plant foods or preparing leather for clothes or bags. People's ingenuity no longer had any bounds and throughout the world they showed themselves capable of intelligent ways of obtaining their food from almost any source. The Bushman bow and arrow is an excellent example of such skill.

5 • Howiesons Poort •

The Middle Stone Age was a time of increasing experimentation by early modern people, *Homo sapiens*, who were becoming more and more like ourselves, *Homo sapiens sapiens*. At Howiesons Poort, near Grahamstown, a distinct stone tool culture has been recognised, dated to around 70 000 years ago. This included tools made from stone brought in from some distance. Flakes of stone were struck off a core in the form of blades, which were then trimmed to make smaller tools. At Peers Cave in the Fish Hoek Valley, the Howiesons Poort industry was found above (and so was younger than) a Middle Stone Age flake industry. But it seems to have lasted only for around 10 000–15 000 years before it was succeeded once more by a flake industry using local stone. In other words, the Howiesons Poort period was one of trial and error which was only partially successful and did not continue, although such experiments in flaking would be found again, 20 000 years ago in the Later Stone Age.

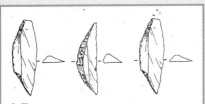

2.7: *Howiesons Poort artefacts showing the first use by archaic* Homo sapiens *of slender blade implements, which would become common in the Later Stone Age.*

CHAPTER THREE

The Later Stone Age archaeology of South Africa

Hunting people have existed in southern Africa continuously until the present time. We can therefore be quite confident that the Later Stone Age people who lived here 20 000 years ago were the direct ancestors of the modern Bushmen.

Over these many years the material culture of hunting society changed. We know this from the kinds of stone tools that were made. Equally, the environment was not always the same as today, so foragers had to adjust to the plants and animals available to them. Hunting and gathering people are quick to take advantage of any opportunity offered to them, and they will adapt to using the resources in almost any environment. Sometimes environments changed to such a degree, however, that they became inhospitable to human existence and survival, and consequently people would have moved away until conditions improved.

An example of this comes from Elands Bay Cave on the western Cape coast: there is a gap in occupation between 8000 and 4000 years ago when the cave was not occupied. This is consistent with other sites on the coast. We do know that people were living in the mountains at this period. Possibly the coast was too dry and difficult for human life, and they left for the interior where life was much easier.

Inland hunters

Caves are the main sources of information in the South African interior. Although many open sites have been found, they were often occupied for such short periods that until recently, because of their small size, archaeologists did little work on them. Because cave sites often have long periods of use going back many thousands of years, they have been very attractive for archaeological research, and a number of them are dry enough to preserve organic remains, which usually disintegrate very quickly.

Just such a cave was excavated by the archaeologist Hilary Deacon at Melkhoutboom in the mountains some 60 kilometres west of Grahamstown. This site was occupied from before 15 000 years ago up to the pottery period (within the last 2000 years). The preservation was so good that recovery was made of leather fragments with stitching, sinew cord, fibre string and netting, fragments of reed arrow-shafts, fire-sticks, wooden pegs, plant food remains, as well as a number of bone artefacts.

Many plant species were also identified, some of which were edible, such as *Watsonia* and *Hypoxis* bulbs which, when cooked, taste like potatoes. The early European travellers wrote about the Bushmen digging for *uintjies* (small onions). So plentiful were these in the late summer that a woman could probably harvest enough for her family's daily needs with less than an hour's work.

A number of the plant remains found at Melkhoutboom were used as medicines, or were poisonous and used as arrow poison (*Boophane*), while others were employed for fibres. This rich site gives us excellent information on the wide range of materials used by these hunting people, and tells us what good botanists they must have been.

The Bushmen were very knowledgeable about the uses of plants. Not only did they know which were important food sources, but also which had medicinal properties. From the excavations at Elands Bay Cave, 25 species of plants were identified. At De Hangen, a cave in the mountains of the

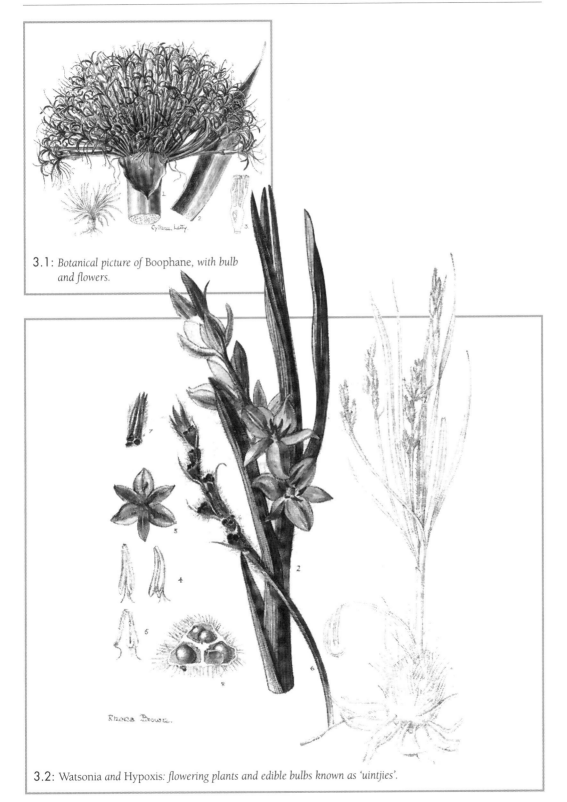

3.1: *Botanical picture of* Boophane, *with bulb and flowers.*

3.2: Watsonia *and* Hypoxis: *flowering plants and edible bulbs known as 'uintjies'.*

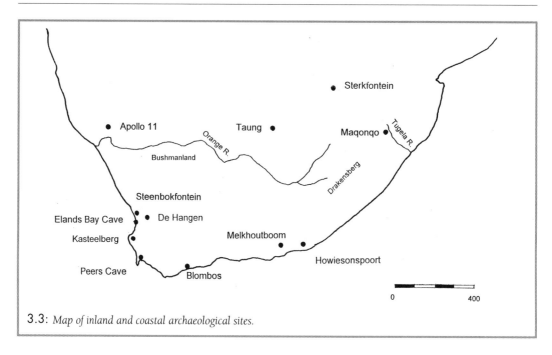

3.3: *Map of inland and coastal archaeological sites.*

6 • Storage of seal and whale meat •

There are historical records of coastal people burying whale meat in the sand. Archaeologists assumed this was to store it, so they did an experiment to find out whether this was very effective, and for how long the meat would last. A newly killed seal was donated by the Marine Mammal Division of Sea Fisheries. The seal was cut up into twenty-five 2-kilogram 'packages' of meat with fat, which were buried in the beach sands along the west coast of the Cape Point Nature Reserve. Five samples were buried in a line extending from the dune above the beach down to the waterline. With 25 samples there were five such lines.

After one day the archaeologists went back and dug up the first line. They found that only the samples in the damp sand in the middle of the beach above the tidal surge zone kept their form as meat. The hot dry dune sands rotted the meat quickly, and in the surge zone they got washed away. The samples were taken to the Fishing Industry Research Laboratory where the bacterial levels were analysed.

The archaeologists continued to take samples at 3, 7, 15 and 21 days. Each day the bacterial counts rose dramatically, but it was only between 15 and 21 days that the meat lost its structure and became 'soupy'. It was very smelly, and bacterial counts were enormous, but in spite of this there were no toxins such as botulism. This meant that if your nose could stand the smell, and your stomach flora could deal with the high bacterial counts, the meat could still be eaten safely.

A whale, which has over 20 tonnes of meat, would rot in the sun very quickly. This experiment was able to show that the meat could be preserved for at least two weeks if it was buried in the damp beach sand.

western Cape, 35 species were found, and at Melkhoutboom 28. Work on plant use among the people living in the Richtersveld today by the ethnobotanist Fiona Archer has shown that there are three different categories of plants used: the people consider 70 species to be edible, 40 species can be used for medicines, and an additional 43 species have other uses, such as building and making mats or baskets. This does not include the 14 species used for firewood.

In Bushman society the men were the hunters, going after antelope, while the women were the gatherers of plant foods. In the dry Karoo it was the huge herds of springbok that the men mainly targeted, while at the coast small steenbok bones are the most common on archaeological sites.

For hunters of the interior one of the scarcest commodities was fat. The meat from game animals is very lean, and fat was highly prized and given almost spiritual qualities. For this reason seals and whales, which have a thick layer of fat, were high-ly desirable and may have encouraged visits to the coast.

Coastal foragers

The coastal foragers had the additional advantage of living off marine foods, such as fish, shellfish, crayfish, marine birds, seals and, when they washed up on the shore, whales.

Two different kinds of site have been excavated at the coast: shell middens and cave sites. Shell middens are accumulations of shell left over from human activities surrounding food. These can usually be differentiated from natural accumulations by their position on or behind dunes, and by the selection of species of shellfish gathered. Natural middens contain everything the sea throws up, but human accumulations often have stone fragments and the bones of terrestrial animals, such as tortoises or steenbok, as well. Since the shells come from people camping along the coastline we can

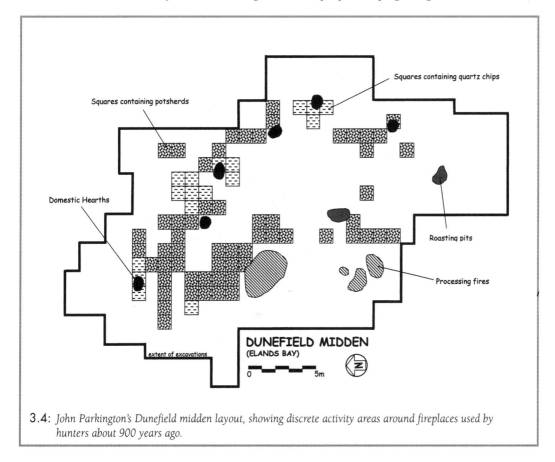

3.4: *John Parkington's Dunefield midden layout, showing discrete activity areas around fireplaces used by hunters about 900 years ago.*

sometimes look at the spatial layout of camps. The best example of this research is John Parkington's work at the Dunefield midden, just north of Elands Bay, on the west coast.

At this site shells and the bones of eland are spatially separated close to fireplaces where the food was cooked. As one can see in Figure 3.4 there is a separation of the distribution of stone (quartz chips) and pottery. Just as in our picnic example in the previous chapter, different activities will leave separate spatial signatures on the ground. At the Dunefield midden, pottery would represent domestic activities such as cooking (possibly women's work), and the presence of stone would show where the making of hunting or scraping tools (possibly men's work) took place. We can see that the processing of shellfish and the roasting of meat were also done at separate locations. Ostrich eggshell beads have also been found. The spatial arrangement hints at separate activities being performed, again possibly on a gender basis, with women making ostrich eggshell beads and men butchering the meat. There are several shell 'dumps', indicating that the people were involved in cleaning up their living space.

While the bones of dolphins were found on archaeological sites, for a long time archaeologists could only assume that people living along the coast would also eat the larger whales. Whale bones are so big that they could not be carried on to sites. But a surprising find was made on shell middens by the archaeologist Chopi Jerardino, who recognised barnacles (*Coronula* sp.) that only grow on the face of whales, such as Humpback or Southern Right whales – they are specific to these large animals, and are not found elsewhere. Since then, they have been found on several other shell middens, indicating that the pieces of whale skin to which the barnacles were once attached had been brought back to the sites.

Coastal foragers also used caves. These have shell middens as well, since the people would carry the shellfish back to their sites, often several kilometres inland. This is where we find occupation and use of coastal resources over a long period of time, and can get information about changes

---

• Estimating diet from human skeletons •

'We are what we eat.' What we eat is broken down by the digestive system, and then absorbed by the other parts of the body, including the skeleton. Human skeletons are therefore a record of our diet, and this can be measured.

Carbon is an important element which makes up a large part of our bodies. We absorb carbon from everything we eat, both meat and vegetables. Plants, however, have different carbon ratios depending on how they get their energy from the sun. These are called 'photosynthetic pathways'.

The pathway of plants adapted to warm, dry conditions is called C_4, and these plants contain relatively large amounts of the stable isotope form of carbon, Carbon-13. Examples of this type would be summer rainfall crops like maize, millet or sorghum. People eating marine foods, such as shellfish, exhibit an average signature close to C_4 plant eaters.

The pathway of plants adapted to cold, wetter conditions is known as C_3 and these contain much less Carbon-13. An example would be underground bulbs in the western Cape.

The skeleton of a person who has eaten C_4 plants or marine foods would exhibit relatively large amounts of Carbon-13, quite different from that of a person who had eaten C_3 plants. People eating the plants directly, or animals subsisting off these plants, would demonstrate quite different isotopic signatures, depending on whether they were inland (eating underground bulbous plants) or at the coast (eating marine foods). From this we can make an estimate of the amount of these foods in the diet, and an inference about whether the people were getting their food inland or from the coast.

in lifestyle which often reflect changes in the environment. For example, at Elands Bay the Verlorenvlei estuary was not always the same as it is today. Some 12 000 years ago the sea was much lower, because of the glacial periods when the polar icecaps were several times their present size. This meant that at Elands Bay the coastline was 25 to 30 kilometres further away than at present. But around 5000 years ago the mean sea level was two metres higher than it is today.

Along with the changes in estuarine conditions went changes in the kinds of fish being caught and eaten by the occupants of the cave, and the bones they left there. Some of the fish bred in the estuary, while others came from deeper water outside. All these fish types give us clues as to conditions in the estuary in the past, and since it is possible to date the different levels in the midden from which the fishbones in the cave came, we also know when the changes took place.

The list of animals recognised from their bones at Elands Bay Cave is a long one and includes both marine (seals, sea birds, crayfish, fish) and terrestrial (antelopes, tortoises, mongooses) – virtually all the animals that would have lived in the area before colonial settlement.

John Parkington has studied sites at the coast, around Elands Bay and in the mountains of the Olifants River drainage. In one of the mountain sites, called De Hangen, he excavated black mussel shells wrapped in the leaves of a bulbous plant. This was an indication that people living in the cave were in contact with the coast. He also found many young dassie bones. Since dassies are all born around the same time in October, it was possible to establish, by examining the teeth of the archaeological sample, that most of the animals had died between the months of September and February. In addition, there were many fragments of the inedible parts of the bulbs of the Iridaceae, which are best collected during the months from September to March.

From these pieces of information Parkington was able to suggest that the site was used during the summer months. He argued from his work at Elands Bay that the obvious place for people to have been during the rest of the year was at the coast. He called this a 'seasonal mobility hypothesis'.

A subsequent study by Judy Sealy and Nick van

8 • Saldanha footprints •

For a number of years archaeologists have been working around Saldanha Bay and the Langebaan Lagoon, but it is only recently that several depressions in the sandstone near the Preekstoel were identified as human footprints. Dating of the rock is difficult, but a good estimate is that they were formed before 100 000 years ago, and would have been made by early modern humans (*Homo sapiens*). There is no question that these people walked upright, just like ourselves, with the big toe fully in line with the other toes. They would have been part of a Middle Stone Age cultural group. Across the bay, at Hoedjiespunt, just such an occupation level with Middle Stone Age stone tools has been found, as well as a fossil carnivore (hyena?) lair. Here the bones of the early humans are mixed with those of antelopes, indicating that these humans were part of the carnivores' diet.

der Merwe looked at the isotopic signature (see Box 7) in the human bones from both Elands Bay and the mountains. They deduced that the coastal skeletons were of people who had spent almost all the year at the coast, and that the inland people had very little seafood in their diet.

The interpretations of these two studies were seemingly in conflict with each other. Re-evaluation of the evidence tells us that the idea of great numbers of people moving seasonally between the west coast and the interior may have been too simple. It is possible, however, that some people from the coast visited the interior, and vice versa. The isotopic readings could indicate territories where coastal people kept mostly at the coast, and suggest that inland people stayed mostly in the mountains but with short forays to the coast, bringing back items like shells. The territories probably changed through time as political alliances shifted. This tells us that human activities are never the same over long periods, and changes in social groupings can restrict people's movements.

There are only a few early written descriptions of people subsisting off coastal resources. One of the more detailed is that of Colonel Robert Gordon, who visited the mouth of the Gariep (Orange) River, and noted in his diary entry for 20 August 1779:

'There was a large hut, made differently from the Hottentots, with two high doors ... open to the E, of wood from cast-up trees, and Noordcaper or whale bones covered with grass and vegetation, and very hot. In it were nine or ten sleeping-places where the skins of rock rabbits and jackal lay. The other hut was smaller and had only one opening, and another smaller, but [with] sitting places, all in a row and attached, so that one wall served for two. In the huts hung sacks of hide and *canna*, or Cape eland horns with buchu and fat, and a baked earthenware pot, as well as many ostrich eggshells, some empty, others filled with a supply of water; and the fire [was] in the middle of the hut which was not high enough for one to stand upright in it. In front of the door they had planted dry cast-up trees, on the branches of which hung pieces of raw whale-meat which had been cut off [and] which they roast or cook as food. We also found two beautiful tanned sealskins.'

Gordon goes on to describe the people who were living in the huts:

'These folk were like the Bushmen in shape, size, clothing, etc., but their teeth were short and bad and ground down [probably from the grit in shellfish diet]. In ... nets their women carried ostrich eggshells filled with water, and wood. I counted one who carried twenty-four full shells on her back ... Two women had the first joint of the small finger on the left hand amputated, they said as a result of "making different" [a time of change, such as a death of a husband] or ... in time of illness ... They had curled their woolly hair around wood thorn-knobs ... They had in addition a few beads and copper earrings which they said had passed from hand to hand for a long time already.'

Hut structures made from whale bones have been found along the Skeleton Coast in Namibia. They show similar layouts to those in the Gordon drawing (see Figure 3.5), with whale vertebrae seats, around fireplaces, and scatterings of shells nearby.

Along the Gariep

The Gariep is a green ribbon that wends its way across an arid land. South of the Middle Gariep lies Bushmanland, named because this was where some of the last Bushmen survived independently in cultural groups until the early 1900s. Many sites of hunting people have been found there, mostly

3.5: *A Bushman family at the mouth of the Gariep living in whalebone hut structures in 1779. (Note the whale vertebrae seats and shellfish around the fire.)*

shallow in nature. These had been occupied for short periods of time, because the resources of this dry interior tend to be very patchy as far as plant foods are concerned. We also know that there were large herds of springbok which used to roam widely over this whole area. People who relied on plant food or springbok meat would not spend very long in one place, and only at special waterholes would they camp at the same place regularly.

As this is a land of periodic droughts, a territory would have to give enough food and water to tide a family over the hard times. Territories were probably between 400 and 1000 square kilometres in area. In 1872 the geologist E.J. Dunn travelled across Bushmanland. He describes one of the Bushman encampments thus:

'A circle of bushes with fire-place in the centre. Stuck into the bushes are the digging sticks of the women, the deadly arrows tipped with puffadder poison, and the bow made of Karree wood, famed for its strength and toughness. The string is made of twisted springbok sinews, is very strong, but unserviceable in damp weather. Curious culinary utensils: a dish made from the upper shell of a tortoise; a brush made from the long hairs of a hyena – it is used for "whipping" ostrich eggs in the shell, after breaking a hole in one end by being twisted rapidly round, for eating soup or milk, and also if the weather be hot as a handkerchief for wiping perspiration from the face; spoons made from ribs of gemsbok, used for extracting the flesh from small cucumbers. Half-a-dozen springbok zakkies [small leather bags] … a … new leather gown … on top of an adjoining bush. Many of the old ladies wear a kind of cowrie shell fastened by threads to the centre of their forehead. These ladies are given to painting [their faces].'

Dunn found a large pit which had been dug by the Bushmen to extract soft red ochre which was used for face painting and mixing with fat for rubbing on the body. He saw the Bushmen burning sociable weavers' nests and eating the roasted weavers. He also noted that water was available only a few feet below the surface in dry river beds. This would have been known to the Bushmen.

The Karoo

As an example of how rich the later archaeological heritage of South Africa is, we can use the study conducted by Garth Sampson in the Upper Seacow River Valley in the Karoo between Richmond and Middelburg. This intensive research has produced roughly 16 000 sites within an area of 5000 square kilometres. These range from cave occupations to small open-air campsites occupied for a limited period of time. From this study Sampson has created both a spatial map of site distribution and a chronology of the occupation by hunting people, as well as describing the influences of Khoe pastoralists and colonists.

On the basis of pottery sequences established by Karim Sadr in the western Cape and in the Seacow River Valley, it would appear that the four major vessel types, which are time markers for four periods, are present in both areas. This suggests that, even though the two areas are separated by 600 kilometres, a similar sequence of pastoral immigration took place. The Bushmen obtained pottery from the pastoralists but also made their own fibre-tempered pots. These could have been used to render fat from the bones of animals, such as the springbok, which are notorious for the low fat content in their meat.

Unlike the western Cape where the Khoekhoen survived to interact with the growing colony, the Seacow River Vally had no Khoekhoen when Europeans first entered the area in AD 1770. Khoe pottery consistently disappears from the top of the sequence at several rock shelters, suggesting a regular withdrawal of herders from the valley, leaving the area for hunters. Whether this was due to pressure from the hunters, or because the area was deemed unsuitable for traditional pastoralism, is unclear. Certainly, as will be seen in the historical section of this book, the Karoo Bushmen were able to organise themselves effectively against encroaching European farmers for some time. The later incorporation and dissolution of Bushman society in the Seacow River Valley in the nineteenth century has been well documented by Dennis Neville as part of the project, and conforms to the pattern experienced by the hunters elsewhere in the Cape.

Archaeology of the Tugela Basin, KwaZulu-Natal

A major study by the archaeologist Aron Mazel of hunting and gathering people who lived in rock shelters of the Tugela Basin gives us important information on how social conditions and diet changed through time in this part of South Africa. Mazel has excavated seventeen shelters within the Upper Tugela Basin that were occupied between 7500 and 650 years ago. One of the early sites, Maqonqo, used until 4000 years ago, produced unusually high quantities of ostrich eggshell beads and broken pieces of eggshell, which indicate the site was an important locus for bead manufacture. This is somewhat surprising, as the area today is too wet for ostriches to breed successfully. If the environment has not changed significantly over the past 4000 years, and there is no evidence that it has, the closest source of eggshell would be about 150 kilometres away. Marine shell beads were also recovered here, indicating that the hunters were in contact with the coast.

As other shelters dating from this period do not show the same intensity of bead manufacture, it is possible that Maqonqo was a special activity site. Support for this idea comes from the number of ochre-stained artefacts, as well as rock paintings on the walls of the shelter.

After 4000 years Maqonqo was no longer used, but other sites close by were. Mzinyashana Rock Shelter is only four kilometres from Maqonqo. It was first occupied around 4000 years ago, so it overlaps with the end of the Maqonqo period of use. While there are similarities with the Maqonqo material, and some beads were probably made there as well, there is no evidence of marine shell.

As far as diet is concerned, the dominant animal bones from the sites are those of the smaller antelope, such as klipspringer, grey rhebok and duiker. Few eland bones were found. There was also a small quantity of fishbones.

Around 1900 years ago pottery was introduced to the Tugela Basin; farmers followed some 300 years later. The rock shelters where the hunters continued to live show evidence of interaction between the two groups. Mazel believes that relations were amicable, and that once the farmers were established the hunters obtained their pottery from them. This may indicate a close relationship, with the hunters performing important tasks for the farmers. It is also a time when many more fishbones were found, showing an increased reliance on fish and an improvement in fishing methods.

Simon Hall, who has studied the fishbones, suggests that these people employed hand-held baskets or even valve traps to catch the smaller fish. A greater dependence on fish may have been the result of pressures on other food resources, which began when farmers entered the landscape, and occupied a great deal of the space with their settlements and grazing needs, space that was previously available to the hunters.

Rock art

A more visible part of the archaeology of the Bushmen, and one which more people know about, is the rock art found throughout the mountains of southern Africa. Initial attempts to understand these paintings were fraught with problems, because the painters had all died before anyone thought to try to find out why they were painted. Because many of the paintings depict animals, one reason given for their existence was that they had to do with hunting and magic.

When the archaeologist Patricia Vinnicombe did her important study on the art, and counted the individual animals on the rock walls in the KwaZulu-Natal Drakensberg, she found that the eland was by far the most common. Archaeological excavation, by contrast, showed that the bones of eland were no greater in number than the bones of other antelope. This led to studies of the importance of eland in the beliefs of the Bushmen.

3.6: *Eland paintings in the Drakensberg showing the shading and foreshortening skills of the artist.*

3.7: *Part of the panel of the famous 'White Lady of the Brandberg' from Namibia (the figure holding the 'tulip' was once thought to be a Phoenician woman, but we now know it is a male figure).*

It emerged that these animals were central to several of their rituals, in that the eland was seen as a rain animal. Since rain in a dry land is crucial for survival and regeneration, the eland symbolised fertility. This was taken even further by the Bushmen, who considered eland fat to have strong sexual potency, thus relating the eland to human fertility.

Bushman art has been analysed in detail by David Lewis-Williams, who was able to identify motifs relating to trance activity by Bushmen healers. From this he has developed the 'trance hypothesis', arguing that most of the paintings have to do with ritual healing and are metaphors for the experience of the healers in trance when they visit the lands of the spirits in order to get power needed to heal the social and physical ills of the group. Trancing takes place around camp fires, often at night, and is induced by monotonous clapping and stamp-dancing in the firelight.

During trance the healer's body becomes rigidly bent-forward and his arms extend backwards. The height of the experience is when the healer experiences his power (or *n/um*) rising up his spine in a tingling sensation. In the rock art humans are seen in this bent-forward position.

In trance all normal perception is altered. People become elongated, or become animals, and animal-headed figures with human bodies are seen in the rock paintings. All this is support for the idea that the paintings refer to the trance experience, and therefore have to do with deep meaning in Bushman beliefs.

Having said that the art is trance-related does not mean that at another level we cannot recognise a narrative or the documentation of a real event. Some of the Drakensberg paintings, for example, show raiding scenes with whites firing their guns at Bushmen stealing cattle. In the Western Cape there are scenes of many human figures. One of these shows men clad in karosses, while nearby are unclad figures. This has been interpreted as a boys'

3.8: *Possible initiation ceremony of young men. The figures wearing karosses are probably older men, while the naked kneeling figures on the right are the initiates.*

initiation ceremony (Figure 3.8).

Other sites show a preponderance of female figures, suggesting that they may have been done for or during a young woman's initiation.

Not every cave is painted, which implies that those caves with rock paintings had special significance. The archaeologist Janette Deacon went to the homeland of the /Xam Bushmen in Bushmanland and was able to show that certain features in the landscape were incorporated into /Xam stories. Since the stories are complex creations of belief, allegory and metaphor about the world of the Bushmen, they contain elements of myth. One such story tells about the lizard who was cut in half when he tried to squeeze through the mountains. The front of the lizard became the western hill of the Strandberg, while the hind part became the eastern hill. Thus the lizard has a physical presence in the form of these mountains, suggesting that some places were more important than others, probably because of their spiritual power.

Paintings are not the only visual art form. Engravings are found in the more arid areas where there are few caves, such as Bushmanland. These are done on large, wind-polished boulders, and are either in the form of thin lines incised into the surface patina, or pecked by hammering with a stone. There are indications that the engravings may also have been part of trance symbolism, but this is less evident than in the paintings.

Bushman paintings or engravings are found throughout southern Africa, and may well stretch as far north as Tanzania. In the major areas such as Zimbabwe, Namibia, the KwaZulu-Natal Drakensberg and the southern and eastern Cape Fold Mountains there are common motifs and ways of depicting animals and humans. However, this general statement does not do justice to the local detail differences, such as fine shading and foreshortening of eland in the Drakensberg, or the strange and enigmatic forms found in Zimbabwe and Namibia.

Another interesting detail is the regional distribution of domestic animals in the art. While cattle depictions are fairly common in the eastern part of South Africa, they are missing from the western Cape, where paintings of fat-tailed sheep are to be found.

9 • Dating rock art •

Putting an age to rock art is notoriously difficult, but is becoming easier with new nuclear accelerator techniques that only use micrograms of organic samples. This has enabled the beginning of early European cave art to be dated to around 30 000 years, although the majority of the best known paintings from such sites as Lascaux in France are around 17 000 years old.

In southern Africa, unfortunately, most of the surviving paintings were not executed with organic pigments (such as charcoal), so we can seldom date them directly. At Apollo 11 Cave in southern Namibia, painted stones come from levels of human occupation with charcoal that gave a date of between 27 000 and 25 000 years ago. In the Western Cape, a piece of painted rock fell off the wall at Springbokfontein, on the west coast. The level into which it fell was dated to around 3500 years ago, which means that the painting must have been done before this date.

Hunters and herders

Around 2000 years ago the first domestic animals appeared in southern Africa. Some animals were transferred to the aboriginal hunting people of the subcontinent, who later became known as the Khoekhoen. This meant that there were three different economic groups: hunter-gatherers who lived by hunting game and collecting food plants; pastoralists or people who relied upon their domestic stock for a good proportion of their diet, but who also hunted; and agropastoral ancestors of the modern Bantu-speaking farmers, whose diet was mostly from the grains they grew in their fields, but who also owned cattle and would hunt on occasion.

These three groups interacted with each other

and, to a limited extent, intermarried when they were in close proximity for long periods. Such marriages, especially between hunters and agro-pastoralists, tended to be unequal. A farmer would take a Bushwoman as one of his wives, but a hunter almost never owned cattle to pay the bridewealth necessary to marry a farmer's daughter. This meant that gene flow from Bushmen to agropastoralist society was one-way.

Bushmen played important roles in agro-pastoralist society as rainmakers, and as hunters of game or collectors of honey, for which services they would be paid, usually in grains or with a sheep. Because Bushman society is very egalitarian, everyone must share, so any animal given as payment would most likely be immediately slaughtered and shared around the camp. This made it very difficult for Bushmen to become herders in their own right. But it must have occurred successfully at some time, otherwise

10 • Early herders of southern Africa •

In the early 1900s it was believed that the Khoekhoen were related to Ethiopian people, who were considered to be the biblical Hamites, and that they had migrated to southern Africa from the Great Lakes region of East Africa. This idea changed when it was recognised that the Khoekhoen were linguistically and genetically related to the Bushmen of southern Africa. Bantu-speaking (Iron Age) people expanding southward were thought to have been the source of domestic animals and pottery, subsequently transferred to the local hunting population. Current work, although it is as yet poorly documented in the archaeological record, hints at the pre-Iron Age existence of sheep in southern Africa. This leads to the possibility that 2000 years ago herding people in East Africa may indeed have passed on domestic stock before the expansion of Bantu-speaking people. The clues to this are in part archaeological – there are signs of domestic sheep and pottery in Namibia and the Northern Province before Iron Age farmers arrived – and in part linguistic: the words for sheep, ram, ox, cattle and sour milk in southern Bantu languages are loan words from Khoekhoe languages, indicating that these animals were in southern Africa before the arrival of Bantu-speaking people.

A recent study of the click languages in eastern and southern Africa by the historian Chris Ehret suggests that there may be a closer connection than hitherto believed, so the transfer of stock to hunters could have taken place much further north than previously considered. It is also possible that non-Bantu-speaking, early pottery-making, herding people of East Africa may have migrated southward through Tanzania, and been instrumental in transferring stock and pottery to the hunters some 2000 years ago. One model is that these commodities trickled down to the western Cape through various hunting groups, who later became the shepherds identified at Kasteelberg. Alternatively, and more likely, in view of the propensity of hunters to slaughter animals immediately so as to share the meat, the animals came to the Cape with immigrating herders from the Northern Province via the Gariep River.

The important point to recognise is that there were sheep in the western Cape before Bantu-speaking, Iron Age people entered southern Africa, and that the forebears of Khoekhoen were the shepherds. The large herds of cattle which later define the Khoekhoen arrived only later (probably around 1000 years ago), and may have come from Iron Age farmers in the eastern Cape. Whether these cattle were brought to the western Cape by a group of people whom we might recognise as Khoekhoen, or were introduced to the shepherds already living there, is an archaeological question that still needs to be resolved.

there would have been no Khoekhoe society.

Herding society expanded into the western half of southern Africa, an area where summer rainfall crops could not grow. The land was useless to agropastoralists, a major reason for Iron Age farmers never moving into the western Cape. It was thus hunters and herders who came to vie for similar resources there. At the coast they both exploited marine animals, while inland the pastures were being competed for by domestic stock and wild game.

The Khoekhoen were historically much more monogamous than agropastoralists, although occasionally a rich chief would have more than one wife. Generally speaking there was little chance of intermarriage between hunters and herders. The idea of separating the two economic groups underlay a recent project to test whether their archaeological signatures were different. Could we recognise hunting sites as being different from herding sites in the western Cape?

Kasteelberg and Witklip

Two sites, completely different from each other, were excavated. Kasteelberg is a koppie, some four kilometres from the shore, with a number of discrete open-air sites around it. Witklip is a large granite dome on the edge of the town of Vredenburg, south of Kasteelberg, where a number of small caves or shelters are to be found.

Excavations at Kasteelberg over a number of years have produced a large quantity of material. As this includes the bones of many sheep, we are confident we are dealing with a herder site. Of some surprise, however, was that seal bones are even more numerous than sheep bones. This led to the conclusion that the site was occupied by herding people performing a specific task: the killing of seals.

The material culture of these herders included many clay pots, but unfortunately these were all broken up into small pieces (around 730 sherds per cubic metre of earth excavated). We know that ostrich eggshell beads were made here: beads were found in various stages of manufacture with an average size of 6 millimetres, and some as big as 11 millimetres. Many bone tools in the form of points and awls were found, and decorative items like ivory bracelets, shell pendants and bone beads

3.9: *A UCT student demonstrates how the grooves at Kasteelberg were used.*

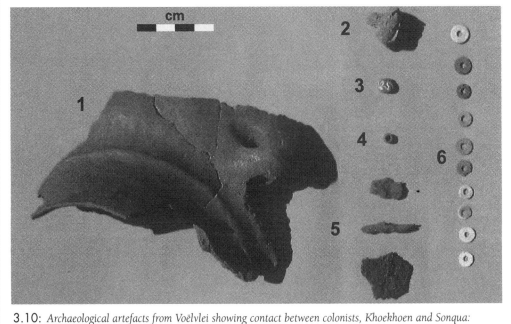

3.10: *Archaeological artefacts from Voëlvlei showing contact between colonists, Khoekhoen and Sonqua: 1. potsherd showing rim and lug; 2. lead shot; 3. glass trade bead; 4. copper bead; 5. pieces of iron; 6. large ostrich eggshell beads.*

showed the importance placed on ornamentation. What was missing were finely made stone tools. All the stone tools found were just crude flakes used for cutting, except for upper and lower grinders from the excavations, which all had ochre staining on them. Around the site we located almost 150 boat-shaped grooves roughly 25 cm long, formed by grinding in the granite bedrock (see Figure 3.9). These marks are identical to those on the portable grindstones found in the excavation.

Witklip is a contrast in many ways. At first glance the material from the excavation looked similar to that of Kasteelberg, but closer analysis showed great differences. The first difference was in the stone tools. Witklip produced some tiny, finely flaked pieces that could have been used as the tips of arrows. The ostrich eggshell beads were small in comparison with those from Kasteelberg, being around 3–4 millimetres in diameter. There were very few potsherds, and of these none of the decorated rims were from the same pot, showing that individual pieces from different pots were being carried on to the site.

The economic differences lay in the kinds of animals represented by their bones. Very few seal

bones were found, although the site is only nine kilometres from the sea. One could argue that this was too far to bring seals back, but another Kasteelberg-type site, called Heuningklip, is 13 kilometres from the sea, and it had plenty of seal bones. The Witklip faunal sample was dominated by small antelope (steenbok). There were a couple of sheep, but these were obviously of less importance than the hunted animals.

It would seem that we were dealing with two quite different archaeological signatures, and subsequent work at other sites in the area has tended to support this separation. The differences in ostrich eggshell bead sizes is significant. Comparing the lower levels of Witklip with Kasteelberg, there is virtually no overlap. In the upper levels of Witklip, dated between 500 and 350 years ago, we do see some overlap, with a few larger beads showing up. From a small rock shelter against the mountains at Voëlvlei Dam, dated to around 400 years ago, we find large ostrich eggshell beads in association with finely made stone tools similar to those from Witklip. From the surface came glass beads and part of a Dutch copper button (Figure3.10).

The upper part of Witklip and Voëlvlei would seem to indicate some cultural overlap. About 500 years before the first appearance of Europeans, cattle increased in considerable numbers. This would have changed the entire cultural and economic landscape of the western Cape. Cattle are a dominant sign of wealth. Any social distinction that had previously been seen between hunters and shepherds would have been exaggerated once cattle began to dominate the herder economies.

Hunters would have found it even more difficult to compete with herders, as they were pushed more and more on to the periphery of pastoral society.

Equally, those hunters who retained links with herders would have been seen as a distinct 'underclass' of stockless people needed as labour, much like the Basarwa of Botswana today, within an increasingly more rigid hierarchy. It is quite possible that the large ostrich eggshell beads found in the later hunter sites are an indication of the induction of hunters into the more dominant society, with these lower-class people taking on some of the cultural attributes of their masters.

The archaeology of hunters and herders shows that each retained their cultural exclusivity, but changes in relationships can be inferred from the material culture remains through time, with the hunters being increasingly dominated by the more structured hierarchy of Khoekhoe society. This is the picture which emerges from the earliest descriptions of the 'Soaqua' by European settlers in the 1600s.

CHAPTER FOUR

Finding the Bushmen in what Europeans wrote

So far this book has been about how archaeologists investigate the Bushmen. We have seen how they excavate sites to find and analyse material which these hunter-gatherers left behind. In this chapter we look for Bushmen in written documents. Most of these are kept in libraries and archives and include accounts by government officials, travellers, missionaries and the colonists who settled amidst – and ultimately incorporated, dispersed or destroyed – the aborigines of the subcontinent.

Identifying Bushmen in the historical record (1488–1800)

As we have seen, hunter-gatherers harvested marine resources at coastal sites during part of the year. The coastal belt was also used by Khoekhoe herders, from Namibia to the Eastern Cape, where there were pastures for their herds and flocks. By chance, the first recorded European contact with the indigenous people of southern Africa was with stock-keepers at the coast. In 1488, when the Portuguese explorer Bartolomeu Dias and his crew came ashore near Mossel Bay, they met herders. This was a welcome event as the mariners saw a chance to replenish their stores by bartering with the herders for fresh meat.

The next contact, nine years later, was made with people without stock. When the Portuguese captain Vasco da Gama dropped anchor in St Helena Bay he saw 'swarthy' men who 'eat only sea-wolves and whales and the flesh of gazelles and the roots of plants'. The Portuguese landed on the beach and captured one of these men. 'He was small of body, and … was going about gathering honey on the moor …' No sheep or cattle were seen.

Although the Europeans noticed differences between the groups of people whom they met, it appears that no one rounding the Cape *en route* to the East, during the next century and a half, identified two different ways of life. Jan van Riebeeck, the commander of the Dutch settlement on Table Bay, was the first to systematically observe and classify the Cape inhabitants.

Three Khoekhoen – Autshumato (called 'Harry' by the Dutch), Doman, and Krotoa ('Eva') – were Van Riebeeck's chief interpreters and informants. According to their information the local people fell roughly in two groups: the keepers of livestock and the robbers of livestock. A middle group, called Fishermen, was said to have a few animals. Confusion arose from the news that Fishermen, who sometimes were called Sonqua, would 'bring us cattle for sale … they lived on nothing else but what they stole'. Autshumato and other herders had informed the Dutch that the Sonqua were without cattle, and were the implacable enemies of livestock owners. The fact that Fishermen, or Sonqua, were sometimes found with stock muddled the neat categories which the Europeans sought to impose.

In 1655, a Dutch party came across 'a certain people of very small stature, subsisting very meagrely, quite wild, without huts, cattle or anything in the world, clad in small skins like these Hottentots and speaking almost as they do'. This appears to have been the settlers' first contact with archetypal 'Bushmen'.

Throughout Van Riebeeck's tenure of office (1652–62) and beyond, Bushmen were characterised by pastoralists as enemies and thieves. Nevertheless, forms of co-operation existed too. The Dutch observed that 'Sonquas' served the

4.1: *Peter Kolb, a German visitor to the Cape in the early 1700s, created a pictorial record of Khoesaan lifeways. Although we cannot be certain he correctly identified the people he labelled 'Hottentots' or 'Bosjesmen', his drawings of their activities, like this one titled 'Hoe zy de Visschen vangen' (How they catch fish), are probably accurate. In 1811 the traveller W. J. Burchell described two young Bushmen 'standing at the water's edge as motionless as herons. After patiently waiting more than half an hour, one of the fishes came within their reach, and with unerring aim, was instantly pierced through with their hassagay.'*

Khoekhoen as scouts, soldiers and even herdsmen in return for protection and food. The Dutch themselves met Bushmen who acted as guides, bartered items such as honey, roasted dassies and dried fish for tobacco, nursed ill explorers back to health, and agreed to provide 'young horses' (zebras or quaggas which the settlers believed might be of use, as they had no horses when they first arrived). Later on, Bushmen guarded the settlers' livestock faithfully, as they had done for the Khoekhoen. Co-operative arrangements, where subordinates retain more independence than a servant normally enjoys, are called 'patron–client' relationships.

During the 1600s certain stereotypes concern-ing Bushmen became fixed in the Europeans' minds. They interpreted the hunters' dependence on wild foods, and their scant material posses-sions, as signs of misery and deprivation. Because the Bushmen spoke a strange explosive language, had no familiar form of government and – know-ing nothing of the Christian God – practised mys-terious rituals, the Europeans described them neg-atively, using words such as 'depraved'. When Governor Simon van der Stel travelled to the Copper Mountains in Namaqualand in 1685, his expedition met Sonqua who 'were all very thin and lightly built, owing to the great hunger and hard-ship they suffer. They eat only the bulbs of a flower which they call ajuintjes, and tortoises, and certain

11 • What is 'identity'? •

Identity is not as simple as it may appear at first. People have identities as individuals, and also as members of a group or groups. People receive an identity when they are named at birth – but birth names may be replaced in later life, for example at initiation or on marriage. The changes may be volun-tary, or they may be forced.

Here is how some Bushmen near the Zak River received new names from the mission-ary J.J. Kicherer, around the year 1800: 'the Boschemen flocking to us in considerable numbers, we were obliged, for the sake of dis-tinguishing one from another, to give them names, which I wrote with chalk on their backs: accordingly when any one of them approached me, the first thing he did was to show me his shoulders.' These Bushmen had names already, which Kicherer found difficult to spell and to pronounce. But the missionary was probably aware that names and identity are very close. By giving them new names he was taking a first step in transforming the people he had come to teach, from 'heathens' into Christians.

People seek identities beyond themselves, in groups. They may identify with a political party or religious community and, beyond that, with a nation or a continent. But people may also be placed in groups not of their choice. South Africans experienced this when they were classified according to 'race' for the apartheid government's Population Register.

Creating identities by describing and classi-fying people, and assigning them to groups, has a long history. Before people from Europe reached the Cape, the herders (Khoekhoen) saw the hunter-gatherers as different from themselves and gave them names like 'Sonqua' (see Box 1 in Chapter 1). At the start, when everything was strange to them, the Europeans used interpreters to help them sort the indigenous people into groups. They combined this information with their own impressions when they ventured inland and met people face to face. This chapter will trace the steps by which the Europeans defined 'Bushmen', as different in important ways from 'Hottentots'.

The quest to classify can never be com-plete. People reshape their identities, and move in and out of groups. Was this farm-worker angry or resigned – or amused? – when he remarked (in 1994): 'I am not a black man and I am not a white man. I must be a Bushman.'

4.2: *The English artist Samuel Daniell, who accompanied the Somerville–Truter expedition to the Cape interior in 1801, captured much detail in his drawings. Note the huts, dress, weapons and other artefacts included in this depiction of Bushmen frying locusts, a plentiful and favoured food.*

large caterpillars, as also locusts, which are found here in abundance. H[is] E[xcellency] had a sheep killed for them, and cooked with bread and rice … [and gave them brandy after which they danced] singing and shrieking in a very strange manner, to be compared only with a party of yearling calves just let out of their stable. It was undoubtedly, as also by their own admission, the only joyful day that they had passed in all their life.'

Were these hunter-gatherers' lives as joyless as Van der Stel believed? Anthropologist Marshall Sahlins has pointed out that, just because people eat things which outsiders find repugnant, we should not assume that food is scarce and they are struggling to survive. According to the anthropologist Richard Lee, many foragers are able to support themselves with very little work.

'Bushmen' with livestock, 'Hottentots' without

Identifying Bushmen became more complicated as the expanding European settlement disturbed the earlier relationships and ways of life. The Europeans had identified Bushmen as of the same 'race' as the Khoekhoen, but distinct from them on economic grounds. These definitions held fairly firm in the 1700s.

The Swedish traveller Anders Sparrman in 1775 described 'another species of Hottentots, who have got the name of *Boshies-men*, from dwelling in woody or mountainous places. These … are sworn enemies to the pastoral life … and are pursued and exterminated like the wild beasts, whose manners they have assumed.'

12 • Interpreting the historical record •

Written historical records give the impression that the interests of hunters and herders were usually opposed. This agrees with what anthropologists have observed in modern populations. It is generally agreed that Bushmen (who were not themselves herders) retaliated against pastoralists wherever hunting grounds and water sources which they used had been taken over and their survival threatened.

This reading of the evidence has been challenged. The historian Yvette Abrahams has argued that, faced with a European presence, the spokespersons for the herders purposely misled the intruders by attributing livestock theft and refusal to trade to a (fictional) group of cattleless thieves. Once this notion had been implanted, the Dutch identified those aborigines who appeared to be 'well armed and had no cattle' as 'Soaquas', without checking that idea against the facts. Abrahams believes that this policy, adopted by certain herders, should be seen as a strategy to deflect the colonists' reprisals from themselves.

In *The Cape Herders* we said: 'The written records are not waiting for a perfectly objective historian who will tell us, finally, what they mean. They are resources: new questions will yield new information and analyses which challenge our ideas.' Abrahams's analysis illustrates the way in which the written records can be reinterpreted. She claims that some historians have been guilty of 'an improper use of sources', as a result of assumptions of which they were unaware. A different interpretation results when documents (like the *Journal* of the Dutch East India Company) are read from the perspective of 'the strategies and aims of the Khoisan'.

How do historians respond to Abrahams's challenge? They may ignore or just dismiss what she has proposed; they may restate, or find new evidence which refutes her theories; they may think that her insights are important, and build on them in various ways. The way we understand the history of the Khoesaan may, or may not, be changed.

But Bushmen with domestic stock, like the Fishermen mentioned above, were often seen. In 1689, Ensign Isaq Schrijver explored eastwards in search of cattle-rich Khoekhoen, called Inqua, of whom the Dutch had heard. Schrijver claimed to have seen several parties of 'Sonquas' who had sheep and cattle.

Again, at the Sundays River, Sparrman found 'three old Hottentots … They were, properly speaking, of the race of *Boshies-men*, though of the more civilized sort, who, even in their own language, distinguished themselves by the name of *good Boshies-men*; probably from the circumstance of their grazing a few cattle, and not living by rapine like others of their countrymen.'

Who were these people?

In 1705 Landdrost Johannes Starrenburg of Stellenbosch had deplored the greedy exploitation of the system of cattle bartering which the Company had allowed, whereby 'Hottentots … [who formerly] sustained themselves quietly by cattle-breeding … [had] become Bushmen, hunters and brigands, dispersed everywhere' and, being so extremely poor, were living by hunting with the assistance of 'their Sonquas (or soldiers)'. Even Sparrman was not sure what name belonged to the three old men he came upon. Debates about the lifestyles of, and the relationships between, the hunters and herders have continued to the present day.

In the late 1700s a massive struggle waged by people frequently described as 'Bushmen-Hottentots' turned back, or contained for almost thirty years, the penetration by colonists of the hinterland. Some historians believe that many of these people were impoverished Khoekhoen who had been forced to live like Bushmen. On this point Nigel Penn has claimed that the frontier

13 • First-hand accounts? •

When historians investigate earlier writings they sometimes find that they were not based upon the first-hand observations of the writer. Stories heard from colonists were passed on to (mainly European) readers as if the writers knew, out of their own experience, that they were true. These stories were copied, or used as if they were their own ideas, by later writers and spread more widely in the guise of first-hand information. Here are some examples:

• 1813 John Campbell: 'The name Bushmen perhaps originated ... 1st. From their country ... being almost destitute of trees, but much of it being covered with bushes: 2d. From their method of assault, as they never attack man or beast openly but from behind bushes.'

• 1820 Barnabas Shaw: 'The race of people called Bushmen, are thus designated from the place of their residence, which is among the bushes; or from the concealed manner in which they make an attack either to kill or plunder.'

• 1799 James Kicherer: Bushmen were 'total strangers to domestic happiness ... [and] will kill their children without remorse ... as when they are ill-shaped, when they are in want of food, when the father of a child has forsaken its mother, or when obliged to flee from the Farmers or others ... There are instances of parents throwing their tender offspring to the hungry Lion ... Many of these wild Hottentots live by plunder and murder, and are guilty of the most horrid and atrocious actions.'

• 1820 Barnabas Shaw: 'The Bushmen are altogether the slaves of passion. They are deeply versed in deceit, and treacherous in the extreme ... Cruelty, in its most shocking forms, is familiar ... Hottentots seldom destroy their offspring ... but the Bushmen will kill them on various occasions, as, when they are in need of food; when obliged to flee from their enemies; when the child is ill-shaped; or, when the father has forsaken its mother ... There are also instances of parents throwing their children to the hungry lion, when he has approached their residence.'

---

farmers perceived 'Bushmen-Hottentots' as Bushmen, by and large, rather than as former herders. Bushmen could still be readily distinguished from the Khoekhoen, and the colonists adopted different policies towards each when they tried to quell their resistance.

Penn's analysis follows a careful study of all the records – official and other – which he could find. It contrasts with the impression we might get, where Bushman identity is concerned, if just a single source is used.

Here is what the traveller François le Vaillant, who toured the Cape during 1781–5, led his European readers to believe: 'These vagabonds [the Boshis-men] are not ... a particular nation of savages ... they are a collection of Mulattos, Negroes, Bastard-whites and, sometimes, Hottentots; mongrels of all kinds, and every shade of colour, resembling each other only in treachery and villainy ...' Was Le Vaillant, who formed his impressions while the frontier war was going on, reporting what he actually saw? Or did he, perhaps, reflect feelings which the war had aroused?

A debate: Bushman identity in the 1800s – and today

At the same time that many Bushmen (or Bushmen-Hottentots) were fighting to preserve their way of life, others were becoming labourers on the colonists' farms. In 1807 Landdrost Anders Stockenström of Graaff-Reinet informed the Governor that most of the 'Hottentot' labour force in his district was 'generated from the Bosjesmen'. In 1822 his son, Andries Stockenström, who was the landdrost by that time, repeated the claim: 'captured Bushmen ... at length ... are as it were confounded with the Hottentots.' These comments reveal a great deal about what was going on. Bushmen were being 'captured' and made to work for colonists. Those who remained in service were being lumped with the Khoekhoen.

As the historian Susan Newton-King has pointed out, 'Hottentot' had become 'both an ethnic and a legal category'. By this she means that the term 'Hottentot' had come to refer to a 'race' which, additionally, was subject to a set of race-specific laws. In the early 1800s, Hottentots were required to carry passes and to enter into labour contracts with employers – but this did not apply to those recognised as Bushmen, who (in Colonel Richard Collins's words) 'enjoy a ramble, and to eat locusts, wild roots, and the larvae of ants' for much of every year.

In 1812, the English traveller William Burchell described an incident in which the Cape people who accompanied him singled out a member of the party (called Keyser), who 'being of short stature, in features not unlike a Bushman, and speaking that language fluently, his companions would sometimes teaze him, by pretending to believe that he was really a wild Bushman who had been caught when young, and brought up in a boor's family. He was, however, a Colonial Hottentot ...'

This story shows a playful awareness by the Khoesaan of the identities which the Europeans had defined. It also shows how persons who record such stories impose their own interpretations ('He was ... a Colonial Hottentot') on the circumstances they describe.

James Kicherer was one of four London Missionary Society (LMS) missionaries who reached the Cape in 1799. Moravian missionaries had founded a mission near Caledon for the Khoekhoen; Kicherer and his partner, William Edwards, were the first to found a mission to the Bushmen. Other missionaries followed.

After they got to know conditions at the Cape, some of the missionaries came to feel that the Khoesaan were shamefully oppressed. Dr John Philip, who arrived as superintendent of the London Society's mission institutions at the Cape in 1819, became the best-known champion of Khoesaan rights. The Cape had no official archives at the time but Philip researched both government and mission papers, and borrowed documents from friends. These sources convinced him of the colonists' longstanding cruelty towards the Khoesaan, which had impoverished and oppressed

them. When Philip campaigned to end the injustices which, he believed, hindered the 'improvement' of the aborigines, most colonists responded angrily. A few agreed. The Scots settler Thomas Pringle reflected Philip's ideas when he explained: 'The Bushmen ... appear to be the remains of Hottentot hordes, originally subsisting, like all the aboriginal tribes of Southern Africa, chiefly by rearing sheep and cattle; but who have been driven, either by the gradual encroachments of the European Colonists, or by internal wars with other tribes, to seek for refuge among the inaccessible rocks and deserts of the interior.'

Philip's book, titled *Researches in South Africa*, coincided with Ordinance 50 of 1828, which conferred civil rights on 'Hottentots and other free Persons of colour'. Many colonists resented his *Researches*; one of these, Donald Moodie, compiled a book called *The Record* in which he tried to disprove certain of the allegations which Philip had made.

Moodie claimed that the hunters – as distinct from herders – had existed long before the Europeans arrived, and 'they were then, as they still are, the scourge of every people possessing cattle'. By this he meant to destroy any theory which traced 'the origin of [the Bushmen] to European oppression'.

The debate which Philip and Moodie began is still alive today. Eyewitness observations, such as that by Starrenburg, quoted above, have suggested to some historians that the Bushmen and the Khoekhoen were not as distinct as many writers have claimed. Richard Elphick came to believe that although 'such a dichotomy must clearly have existed when Khoikhoi first penetrated any new region of southern Africa, it had been greatly blurred by the time whites first came upon the scene'. He proposed an 'ecological cycle', according to which people moved fairly freely between herding and hunting, depending on conditions at a given time.

Yvette Abrahams goes further, denying what she calls the 'myth of the "Bushman."' She rejects the idea that, once herding was an option, there had persisted 'groups ... who were "pure" hunter-gatherers, who had remained in this technological level since the evolution of the species, and whose economic system necessarily pitted them in fundamental opposition to pastoralists'.

4.3: *This picture, titled 'Bushman Family and Hottentot', contrasts a Khoekhoen, who is shown by his clothing as more assimilated into colonial culture, with a group of Bushmen.*

Song of the Wild Bushman

Let the proud boor possess his flocks,
And boast his fields of grain;
My home is 'mid the mountain rocks,
The desert my domain.
I plant no herbs or pleasant fruits,
Nor toil for savoury cheer:
The desert yields me juicy roots,
And herds of bounding deer.

The countless springboks are my
    flock,
Spread o'er the boundless plain;
The buffalo bends to my yoke,
And the wild horse to my rein*:
My yoke is the quivering assagai,
My rein the tough bow-string;
My bridle curb is a slender barb—
Yet it quells the forest king.

The crested adder honoureth me,
And yields, at my command,
His poison-bag, like the honey bee,
When I seize him on the sand.
Yea, even the locusts' wasting swarm,
Which mightiest nations dread,
To me brings joy in place of harm,
For I make of them my bread.

Thus I am lord of the Desert Land,
And I will not leave my bounds,
To crouch beneath the Christian's hand,
And kennel with his hounds:
To be a hound, and watch the flocks,
For the cruel White Man's gain—
No! the swart Serpent of the Rocks
His den doth yet retain;
And none who there his sting provokes,
Shall find its poison vain!

4.4: From Thomas Pringle's *Ephemerides*

* The zebra is usually termed *Wilde Paard*, or wild horse, by the Cape Colonists.

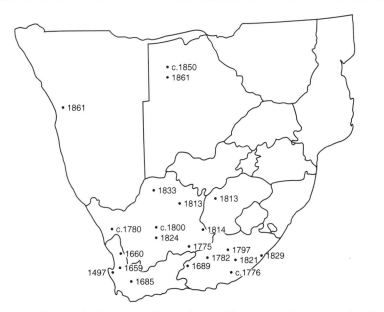

4.5: *Europeans usually noticed and commented on Bushmen while on some other quest, such as for precious metals, fabulous places like Monomotapa, or game to shoot for trophies, hides and tusks. Nevertheless, travellers' journals form a valuable resource regarding the hunters' whereabouts and habits. George Stow, author of* The Native Races of South Africa, *used explorers' accounts to locate what he called the 'various groups of Bushman tribes'. Stow's compilation is the basis for this map, with some additions drawn from other sources. However, Bushmen used, and were familiar with, much larger areas than the spots where the explorers noticed them on any given date.*

Taking a view more or less opposite to Abrahams's, the historian Nigel Penn has argued that any movement into herding, from the hunters' side, was not 'a simple economic adjustment'; it also required abandoning a cherished culture. Significant blurring by herders of the hunter –herder two-way division only occurred well into the colonial period, after the Khoekhoen had been deprived of the resources (pastures, water and live-stock) upon which their economy relied.

Where were the Bushmen when the Europeans came?

Archaeologists, and those who map the rock art which is found widely in southern Africa, know that Bushmen lived throughout the length and breadth of the land. Historians can show that Europeans made contact with hunter-gatherers in 1497 and, after settlement, met 'Soaqua' bands in all the regions which they explored from their base

in the western Cape. But as the colony expanded, the picture changed. Surviving hunter-gatherers were mainly found in the more arid parts of the interior – regions acknowledged as their habitat, as if those were the places they belonged.

The Dutch official Robert Jacob Gordon was told that, after a punitive expedition against some Bushmen, their chief Koerikei shouted from a cliff, 'What are you doing on my land? You have taken all the places where the eland and other game live. Why did you not stay where the sun goes down, where you first came from?' When the farmer asked him if he did not have sufficient country still, Koerikei replied that 'he did not want to lose the country of his birth and that he would kill their herdsmen, and that he would chase them all away … it would be seen who would win.'

In 1779, when Lt. William Paterson visited the Zuurveld, to the east, he learned that it was known as Bushmanland. Before long, the Bushmen's claim had been erased and the driest stretches to the

4.6: *In the early 1800s, Bushman artists painted two figures in European dress, with muskets and horses, at the Caledon River. Are these men colonists – perhaps Col. Richard Collins and another official, as some have speculated – or are they Bushmen who had acquired guns and horses along with colonial uniforms or other clothing? Are the wild animals, including maned lions, part of this drawing or additions by other artists? Interpreting Bushman rock art presents many challenges. (Photo: Sven Ouzman, National Museum)*

north and the north-east appeared on maps as Bushmanland. The inspector of the Cape's LMS missions, John Campbell, observed in 1813: 'It is difficult to ascertain, with any precision, what may be called the Bushmen's country; the people live in so scattered a manner ...'

In 1809, Richard Collins toured the Cape interior in order to advise the Governor how best to end hostilities between the Bushmen and the colonists. Collins denied that the extension of the colony's boundary had aroused 'the enmity of the Bosjesmen ... at being forced by the colonists to quit the territory of their ancestors'. They had always, he maintained, 'resided in the country they now inhabit [beyond the Zak River] since the Cape has been possessed by Europeans'. On present information we can say that Landdrost Stockenström of Graaff-Reinet was much more faithful to the facts when he observed in 1826: 'The encroachments on the Aborigines began at Cape Town, and never ceased to extend by degrees until the colonists had got to where they are now.'

It was once widely believed that Bushman experience was lost to written history. The historian W.M. Macmillan, who wrote about 'Hottentots', regretted that, so far as Bushmen are concerned, 'there is little for history to say'. This is not the case at all. A lot is known not only about living Bushmen but about their lifestyles and interactions with other people, both before and after European colonists arrived.

CHAPTER FIVE

The Bushman way of life – through European eyes

5.1: *When the Somerville–Truter expedition reached the Gariep River, William Somerville described the crossing as dangerous and very difficult: 'an operation which never could have been effected but by the aid of the Bosjiesmen ... they [and also herders called Korana] float themselves upon a dried stem of the willow about eight feet long, in the centre of which a peg is inserted which they lay hold of ... and [swim] with the right hand and both feet. They ferry a sheep over with great facility in this way.'*

People from Europe were keen collectors of information about the Bushman way of life. From the start of the Age of Exploration in the 1400s, Europeans were fascinated by the people of distant lands whose customs were very different from their own. The data they collected formed the basis for ethnography, a branch of anthropology which describes the customs and behaviour of homogeneous groups (sometimes called 'tribes').

When the Europeans contrasted the lifestyle and artefacts of the 'new world' with those of their own societies they used words like 'primitive' – which means ancient, or simple, but came to imply backward, or inferior. Officials and travellers at the Cape described the Bushmen's weaponry, their fish traps, nets and game pits, their shelters, clothing and ornamentation, their manner of preparing and eating food, and their music and dance.

They also attempted to explain the more mysterious aspects of Bushman culture, including their forms of healing and worship, marriage and burial. For the most part, neither Bushman nor Khoekhoen was credited with any notion of religion. David Chidester, professor of comparative religion, has pointed out how, by denying that the indigenous people of newly discovered countries had a religion, the Europeans could justify taking their land. An influential spokesperson made this connection in the 1700s when he said, about the Cape: 'pity 'tis that so beautiful and rich a country should be inhabited by so barbarous and rude a people'.

Some accounts, like R.J. Gordon's description in 1779 of a healing ritual, resemble Bushman practice in the present day: 'Saw an old woman performing sorcery. From her son's body she snorted forth a devil (evil spirit) which she said she could see and it was like a cobra. The snorting made her nose bleed. She walked away drunkenly with the evil spirit. One of them held her under the arms. Quickly she was given a stick which she used to walk on her own. She also beat the ground with it. She snorted once more upon her son's nose. She rubbed his belly with buchu. At the same time some of the women sitting there were smoking buchu through the nose.'

Other accounts are less reliable and illustrate the Europeans' readiness to ridicule exotic peoples.

As with those of the Khoekhoen, Bushman languages were often represented as scarcely human

5.2: *This painting, which the artist Samuel Daniell titled 'Bushmen Hottentots armed for an expedition', depicts hunters who have no cattle, sheep or*

goats. But as archaeologist Pieter Jolly has pointed out, the matjieshuise *in the background resemble Khoekhoe dwellings. Pictures like this alert viewers to the fact that the ethnic groups of southern Africa were in contact with each other and, when it suited, could copy each other's ways of life.*

14 • Bushmen and Aristotle's 'Great Chain of Being' •

As far back as Aristotle, human beings have tried to explain their relationship to other living creatures by ranking them in order of complexity. According to Aristotle's system, 'man' is the highest-ranking animal. Human beings stand between other animals and divine beings (gods, angels), who rank above them all.

In the 1700s the botanist Linnaeus developed a new system for classifying the natural world, which he thought was separate from the divine or supernatural world. His system, which also ranked living creatures in a hierarchy or 'chain', excluded the Khoesaan from the species *Homo sapiens*, and called them *Homo monstrosis monorchidei*.

The Age of Exploration introduced Europeans to people who were very different from themselves; these they called 'savages'. They argued about how to classify such people: Did Bushmen (and their close relatives, the 'Hottentots') rank among the human beings or among the lower animals, or 'brutes'?

1659: Near the Berg River a party of colonists met Soaqua, 'a most barbarous people possessing neither houses nor livestock'.

1696: John Ovington, a mariner who called at the Cape, said about the Khoekhoen: 'of all People they are the most Bestial and sordid. They are the very Reverse of Human kind ... so that if there's any medium between a Rational Animal and a Beast, the Hotontot lays the fairest Claim to that Species.'

1730s: After refuting some of the harsh things that other writers had said about the 'Hottentots', O.F. Mentzel declared: 'Of course, I except those wild Hottentots who are called *Bosmannen* or Bushmen: for these are very much inclined to rob, steal and murder, know of no fixed principle, live scattered about in ravines and rocks, band themselves together only when they wish to attack the tame Hottentots and are a complete contrast to the latter.'

5.3: *Throughout the 1800s, Bushmen were exhibited in Europe. The impresario Farini displayed this group in the 1880s.*

1803–6: The German traveller Hinrich Lichtenstein wrote: 'there is not perhaps any class of savages upon the earth that lead lives so near those of the brutes as the Bosjesmans; – none perhaps who are sunk so low, who are so unimportant in the scale of existence; – whose wants, whose cares, and whose joys, are so low in their nature; – and who are consequently so little capable of cultivation.'

1826: Andries Stockenström reported that the Bushmen near the Gariep River were 'in the lowest savage state, and we shall have gained a great point if we raise them one step by making them graziers, and rendering their subsistence less precarious'.

1853: Charles Dickens despised the 'Noble Savage' in general, and Bushmen in particular: 'he is a savage – cruel, false, thievish, murderous; addicted more or less to grease, entrails, and beastly customs; a wild animal ... Think of the Bushmen. Think of the two men and the two women who have been exhibited about England for some years. Are the majority of persons – who remember the horrid little leader of that party ... conscious of an affectionate yearning towards that noble savage, or is it idiosyncratic in me to abhor, detest, abominate and abjure him?'

and too difficult to be learned. On longer acquaintance, the Europeans became aware of other features of Bushman culture such as their rock art and their reputation as rainmakers. In their descriptions, writers (and painters) were careful to point out differences in Bushman and Khoekhoe culture. This interest led to the creation of a distinctive 'Bushman' ethnography.

When the Europeans identified the Bushman hunters or robbers as separate from, and inferior to, the Khoekhoe herders, they used a system for classifying people. Bushmen, who owned no property and would not 'settle down', were seen as lower in the scale of civilisation than the 'Hottentots', who had livestock and other goods; people who herded and also planted crops were considered to be higher still. When the English traveller William Burchell noted the distinctions of rank and wealth among the Tswana in 1812, he wrote: 'I had hitherto been accustomed among the Bushmen, to see all men on an *equality*; that is, that of the individuals of a kraal, no one possessed more property than another, or, at least, there was not so much difference as to occasion them to make a distinction between *rich* and *poor*. But those tribes are … in the lowest degree of human polity and social existence; and in such only, can all men be on a level with respect to property: or in other words, a nation, to be equal, must, even in the aggregate, possess no property at all; which is precisely the case with the Bushman nation.' Egalitarianism in Bushman society is better understood today.

Another indicator of low status was that Bushmen appeared to be without a 'polity', or government.

Did the Bushmen have chiefs?

An important reason for the early negative depictions of the Bushmen was that, as far as Europeans could make out, they lacked any form of leadership and government. In 1826, Andries Stockenström interpreted this as a major reason

5.4: *The English traveller William Burchell identified these two oxen-riders as 'Tame Bushmen', signifying their adoption of some Khoekhoe or colonial lifeways, when he met them in the Karoo in 1811: 'One of them, who was called their* Captain, *carried in his hand the ensign of his authority, a staff about four feet long, having a large tabular top of brass, on which were inscribed a few words, showing that he had been elevated to that rank by Governor Caledon … these staves … are … handed down from father to son, conformably to the right of inheritance; and the possessor is always acknowledged as the head, and, with the Cape authorities, the lawful representative of his own particular kraal or tribe; and there has, or ought to have, some degree of consideration shown to him by the landdrosts and field-cornets. This … has, in most cases, the effect of securing the allegiance … of these kraals, especially as it is often, perhaps always, accompanied by a certain annual stipend or present.'*

15 • Some Bushmen whom the colonialists called 'chiefs' •

VIGILANT: While the missionary James Kicherer was absent in Cape Town around 1800, 'The Captain of the Boschemen, named Vigilant, had come to our settlement to seize a sheep as his due.' Violence ensued when some of the mission Bushmen defended the station and its property. Kicherer observed that although few of the smaller 'Hottentot' groups had chiefs, 'The Boschemen are rarely without a Chief, who is generally the most cunning or the most daring among his Banditti. His merit lies in being the most bloody murderer among his gang …' Kicherer's opinion that there were many chiefs is the reverse of what most people believe. As he was new to the Cape, one may speculate as to the source of this account, which was produced for English readers.

LYNX and FROLIC: On his way to Zwagershoek near Somerset East in 1809, Colonel Richard Collins came upon 'two Bosjesman chiefs … at a farm on the road … [who] had about 200 of their people at this and a neighbouring farm. Lynx had been one of the most noted depredators … We gave them a few trifles, and prevailed on Lynx to go with a few more to live with a farmer residing more inwards.'

GOEDHART: In 1811, when north of the Gariep, William Burchell met Goedhart, from the Kareeberg, whom he called a chief. Goedhart's 'brother, some years ago, going into the colony to beg tobacco, was wantonly shot … This man … vowed perpetual vengeance and warfare against [the Boers] … and … had carried off a great number of cattle from the colony'. But as the Klaarwater (Griquatown) missionaries and the station's Khoesaan whom Burchell was with were exempt from Goedhart's wrath, 'he came to us in peace' and was given tobacco.

for Bushman weakness in relation to other groups: 'As for the unfortunate Bushmen, they are without chiefs, laws, Government, or organisation of any kind, so that no human power can save them from absorption, either by ourselves, or by some powerful neighbouring nation …'

But were the Bushmen, of every time and every place, in fact 'without chiefs'? The ethnographer George Stow disagreed: 'Many have stated that the Bushmen were entirely without any form of government. This is altogether an erroneous idea; and was probably formed from what the writers saw of the broken, scattered, and half-annihilated tribes which were to be met with along the exposed frontiers, after their fathers had been driven about and hunted for a couple of generations … The Bushman race was evidently, at one time, divided into a number of large tribes occupying tolerably well-defined tracts of country, which they looked upon as their own ancestral hunting-grounds … These branch-tribes were again divided, although they had but one chief, who was looked upon as paramount over the whole territory belonging to the tribe.'

Many Bushman chiefs are named in the written records. Stow compiled a long list – some bearing traditional names ('Hon'ke and Ma'ku-une, Co-ro-ko and Ma'kla), others with Dutch names (Knecht Windvogel, Kwaai Stuurman, Koegel-man), and a few with both (Ow'ku'ru'keu / Baardman). Historians and others debate whether these men (there are few references to female chiefs) were really leaders, or whether the Europeans treated them as such because they needed leaders who would carry out their laws and orders in the various groups.

In his book *Bushman Raiders of the Drakensberg*, John Wright states: 'In the case of the Southern Bushmen, the bands do not seem to have had any chiefs until fairly late in their history, communal affairs being largely regulated by the skilled hunters and older men. In the days before intrusive peoples began to pose a serious threat to the survival of the Bushmen, there would have been

5.5: *On an expedition to the Calvinia region in 1779, Robert Jacob Gordon, commander of the Dutch garrison at the Cape, met two Bushman chiefs, Gronjam and Doerop, with whom he negotiated peace. On this and other journeys, Gordon was accompanied by fellow-soldier Johannes Schumacher, who doubled as an artist.*

no need for a more sophisticated form of government, for even in later times the life of the band was comparatively simple ...'

The suggestion here is that chiefs may have been a response to the pressures introduced by intruders on Bushman territories. In the mid-1800s, when the 'Bushman raiders' of Natal were being squeezed by African and European settlers, they may have selected individuals to serve as chiefs, whereas before they had not felt a need for leaders.

Nigel Penn gives the debate another twist when he suggests that the colonists failed to 'find kraal captains' not simply 'because the San did not have "captains"' who matched their own ideas but also on account of the Bushmen's 'determination to reject unequal terms' when making peace. Those who consented to act as chiefs were awarded official staffs of office. But, as Penn points out, this often happened under duress, as when 'Nicolaas van der Merwe did manage to persuade a certain Joris, from a kraal at the Zak River, to accept a staff of office but only after he had been captured.'

Regardless of the realities of Bushman social organisation, or preferences, officials and colonists gave proof of what has been termed the 'classic colonial need to negotiate with individuals as leaders'.

On 4 January 1779 Robert Jacob Gordon reported making peace with two Bushman chiefs, Doerop and Gronjam, near Loeriesfontein, north of Calvinia. In the painting made of this occasion, no one (except Gordon himself) is distinguished by his rank or dress although Gordon wrote that Doerop impressed him as being like Ruyter, the Hoengiqua chief (see *The Cape Herders*).

Did the Bushmen have chiefs? To answer questions such as this, historians often seek the help of anthropologists. According to the documents historians use, the answer seems to be both yes and no. The Bushmen were often seen in family groups, or somewhat larger parties, in situations where leadership was not required. Yet when danger threatened or they needed to negotiate, a chief or 'captain' was produced. More often than not, the records left by missionaries, colonists and government officials concern the kind of situations which called forth a chief.

CHAPTER SIX

When cultures clash:
Bushmen resist – and adapt

In the course of a scientific exploration of the interior from 1834 to 1836, Dr Andrew Smith collected information about 'native tribes'. According to one informant, 'the Bushmen were [formerly] much less disposed to hostilities … [and] less opposed to each other than they have subsequently been … it was not uncommon for the inhabitants of one district to repair, with the permission of the owners of another, in quest of support when the want of timely rains had rendered their own comparatively unproductive, but now sanction for such a proceeding was never to be obtained … This change he ascribed partly to the invasion and settlement of other tribes who had so circumscribed the Bushman territories that every community found it necessary to guard each district with jealous care … and partly to new causes of enmity arising out of divided feelings in respect to the line of policy to be adopted towards the neighbouring tribes.'

This account of reciprocity among Bushmen conforms with the observations of anthropologists concerning living people. Smith's informant explained how intergroup relations changed when 'Bushman territories' were 'circumscribed'. By 'other tribes' he evidently meant the Khoekhoe herders and black agro-pastoralists, but 'Bastard' and European colonists were also part of the 'invasion and settlement' of which he spoke.

Bushman relations with other indigenous people

We have seen how Bushmen and Khoekhoen interacted in patron–client relationships, in which hunters served the herders as shepherds and mercenaries in return for food and protection. Early travellers along the Gariep reported peaceful co-existence. For example, Bushmen refrained from robbing Khoekhoe stock in return for Khoekhoe tolerance of their free access to wild animals and plants. But the travellers also witnessed endemic conflict between certain groups. This had its roots in the fact that the pastoralists appropriated the resources of the hunter-gatherers for their own use.

Group dynamics changed when herders came under pressure from colonists. Some Khoekhoen allied themselves with the Bushmen. Smith writes about 'hunters and herders combining … as refugees from a burgeoning colony, to avoid being menials'. This is borne out by Le Vaillant's account of a 'Hottentot' deserter from farm labour who became the leader of a group of Bushmen. At first Le Vaillant 'could not understand how he had chosen to live with robbers' but, after a discussion (the 'Hottentot' spoke Dutch), he was convinced that the provocation which these people had suffered justified their actions. Possibly the Bushmen thought that the 'Hottentot's' familiarity with the colony would assist them in their struggle at that point.

Other Khoekhoen allied themselves with fellow pastoralists among the colonists to protect their herds and flocks from hunter-robbers. In 1772, Carl Thunberg saw a group of 59 Bushmen, including women and children, from the Roggeveld in custody of the Khoekhoe captain Kees: 'for a long time [they had] defended themselves, by rolling large stones down upon their enemies … They … asserted that they acted so in their own defence, the Europeans making every year fresh encroachments upon their lands and possessions … These Hottentots were Boshiesmen.' The traveller Sparrman came across a 'Hottentot' in the

6.1: *Relations between Bushman hunter-gatherers and black farmers ranged from cooperation and mutual dependence to war. Here Bushmen are trying to defend themselves from the interior of a cave against attackers.*

service of a colonist, who captured Bushman women and children 'with an intention to take them home to his master for slaves'.

Bushman relations with black agro-pastoralists were equally complex. Among the Tswana, Andries Stockenström found in 1818: 'here, as much as among the Griquas ['Bastards' north of the Gariep], a horrible animosity towards the Bosjesmen … which considers the murder of a Bosjesman, woman, or child, meritorious under any circumstances'. But some women, at least, were taken as wives by commoners and chiefs, and Bushmen filled the important role of rainmakers among the Tswana, Xhosa and others.

Throughout southern Africa, Bushmen lived with and were absorbed into Bantu-speaking groups. Around 1846 the Bushman chief Yele asked a Natal official not to punish him simply because he was a Bushman. He and some other men (several of them also Bushmen) were living

peacefully with Bantu-speaking wives at the mouth of the Mgumbe River, where they were breeding cattle and cultivating crops.

Sotho chiefs were said to use the Bushmen as raiders, to steal stock. The Bushmen lost their protection when the Free State colonists killed or defeated these chiefs. But there were also instances when black agro-pastoralists joined colonists to hunt and destroy Bushman bands. Some co-operated with the Natal government by acting as buffers between the Bushmen and the colonists. The Bushmen remonstrated with and sometimes robbed the Bantu-speakers in the so-called 'barrier locations' established in the foothills of the Drakensberg.

All told, there is much evidence to support Smith's informant when he remarked on the 'new causes of enmity' among the Bushmen due to 'divided feelings in respect to the line of policy to be adopted towards the neighbouring tribes'.

6.2: *Rainmakers, believed to have been of Bushman origin but largely assimilated with the Mpondomise in the eastern Cape by the time this picture was taken in 1886.*

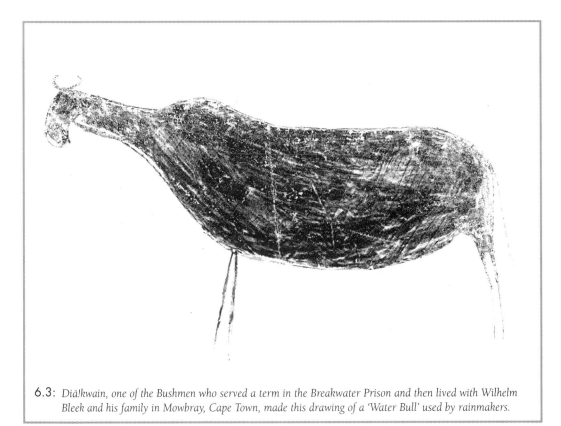

6.3: *Diä!kwain, one of the Bushmen who served a term in the Breakwater Prison and then lived with Wilhelm Bleek and his family in Mowbray, Cape Town, made this drawing of a 'Water Bull' used by rainmakers.*

Bushman relations with the 'Bastards' and the European colonists

The war waged by 'Bushmen-Hottentots' on the Cape's northern frontier between 1770 and 1800 halted the colonists' expansion and forced them to abandon many farms. However, it also led to the death or capture of many Khoesaan. A frontiersman told Colonel Collins that, during six years, 'the parties under his orders had either killed or taken 3,200 of these unfortunate creatures; another has stated to me that the actions in which he had been engaged had caused the destruction of 2,700. They had acted thus in compliance with the instructions of a government ...'

The 'parties' mentioned here were military units called commandos which came into being in the 1700s – at first organised and led by Dutch East India Company officers but, after 1715, by the colonists themselves. They relied heavily on the manpower and the tracking skills of Khoekhoe servants and (in the early days) those Khoekhoe pastoralists still living in a (semi-)independent style. 'Bastards' were also forced to serve in the commandos. As a result of this and other measures, many left the colony and formed communities north of the Gariep.

In 1774 the government responded to Khoesaan incursions on the frontier by ordering a 'General Commando' to subdue and destroy the enemy, wherever found. The precise nature of the orders issued was later disputed. Were the commandos permitted to exterminate Bushmen? Historians have shown that, although the orders to the 1774 commando leaders did not authorise extermination, orders issued three years later did. Despite these measures, the 'Bushmen-Hottentots' advanced or held their ground. The Dutch East India Company seemed at a loss to come to grips with them as the war dragged on.

In 1792 it offered a reward for every Bushman-Hottentot whom the legitimate commandos cap-

---

16 • Andries Waterboer: from Bushman to Griqua chief •

According to Waterboer's biographer, Robert Ross, this 'Griqua' chief was 'said to have been of pure San extraction'. He was born north of the Gariep around 1789 and may have been attached to the household of a leading Bastard family, the Koks (see *The Cape Herders*). As a young man he came under the influence of the LMS missionaries at Klaarwater (later Griquatown) who taught him to read and write, and baptised him in 1807. Waterboer rose through the mission hierarchy, serving as an interpreter and lay reader, until he was suspended on an accusation of adultery. In 1818 he was reinstated in the church, and in 1820 was elected chief – a 'victory for the mission party among the Griquas'.

Waterboer's authority was resented by the older or more traditional Griqua, some of whom broke away and formed rival groups such as the Bergenaars. At first he had the backing of the government of the Cape Colony as well as of the missionaries but in the course of conflicts with his neighbours, and some internal disputes, he forfeited the confidence of both. After beating off a joint attack by Bergenaars and Korana in 1827, he managed to consolidate his chieftainship at last.

In 1834, Waterboer was invited to Cape Town as the first neighbouring head of state to conclude a treaty with the Cape government. In return for arms, ammunition and a money reward, Waterboer engaged 'to be the faithful friend and ally of the colony', responsible for peacekeeping along a section of the Gariep. While alliances with others followed, Waterboer is most prominently linked with this policy initiative.

On his death in 1852, Waterboer was succeeded by his son Nicolaas. After diamonds were discovered in the Griqua state several claimants disputed ownership, which was awarded to Waterboer. The region was then annexed by the Cape.

6.4: *The colonists believed that, although Bushman adults (the men especially) clung to their culture, the children would adopt European culture if they were taken from their parents and brought up by missionaries, or on the colonial farms. This boy is an example of the end-product of such a transformation.*

6.5: *'Wild' Bushman children were captured by colonists, who 'tamed' them by training them as servants. A few, who were handed to the missionaries, were baptised and taught to read and write.*

tured alive. This policy was said to be humane, to save them from extermination, but some frontiersmen misinterpreted it and set up expeditions to catch Khoesaan solely to claim the bounty, fixed at 15 rixdollars per head.

When the British inherited this frontier war, during their first occupation of the Cape (1795–1803), they tried to find new ways to re-establish peace. Lord Macartney, who was Governor for eighteen months during 1797–8, persuaded frontier farmers to distribute sheep among the Bushmen. Looking back (in 1809), Collins reported: 'Since the year 1797, several inhabitants of the north-eastern districts appear to have exerted themselves with as much zeal to acquire the friendship of the Bosjesmen, as they had before done to blot them from the creation ... since the adoption of different measures, they have experienced a degree of tranquillity which they could never before hope for ...'

But the policy was not trouble-free. Hungry Bushmen, who did not have the pastoralists' attitude towards breeding stock, ate the animals which they received and then needed more. Their animals also became the prey of other raiders. Stockenström reported that, in 1818, he had recovered and restored around 2000 sheep and goats which colonists donated to the Bushmen but which black farmers stole. The same frontier farmers were called on, time and again, to donate stock – but not more distant farmers, who also stood to benefit from peace. Collins argued that the distribution of stock had the negative effect – for colonists – of letting Bushmen think they were afraid, and of attracting them from far and wide to the frontier.

It was Collins's belief that missions offered the best hope for bringing Bushmen under colonial control. The project needed strict supervision and steady government support. Mission shops should foster trade by stocking 'such things as the Bosjesmen may wish for', to be exchanged for articles like skins and mats. Bushmen should be denied 'any communication with the colony, except through the missions', which would send 'superfluous inhabitants' into the colony to work.

This proposal, though not carried out, is interesting on several counts. It suggested that there could be no peaceful coexistence so long as the Bushmen kept their culture and their social cohesion, and offered ways and means of altering their way of life. And it was an early indicator of a debate which asks if peace was not more dangerous to Bushman survival than the struggle they were waging, with marked success, even though at considerable cost.

The Bastards, who moved across the Gariep because of their subordinate status to European colonists (as well as for reasons such as their impressment into commandos, noted above), shared many of the practices and values of the colonists. Campbell described a peaceful scene when, in 1813, he met Bushmen 'employed by one of the Griqua captains to watch his cattle, for which service they are allowed to use the milk of the cows, and Bushmen are generally found to be faithful herdsmen'.

But Stockenström implied that the Bastards were harsh masters when, in 1818, he claimed that the Bushmen 'beyond the Orange River are perhaps the most unfortunate beings under the sun', being caught between the Griqua and Tswana. 'A Bosjesman, entering the service of a Griqua, runs as much risk of starving as in his kraal unless he steal, and if he do, he is more sure of death than of his meal.' The traveller George Thompson reported in 1823 how Bushmen annoyed the Griqua and 'other pastoral tribes ... and they are consequently

6.6: *Missionaries and the organisations which supported their work published stories and pictures reflecting their success in winning converts and spreading Christianity. This picture, which was published by the Society for Propagating Christian Knowledge, is titled 'May, the Little Bush Girl'.*

6.7: *Depictions of mission stations featured neatly laid-out gardens, fields and kraals as well as the church, school and European-style dwellings of the missionaries and their flock.*

17 • Andries Pretorius: from Bushman to mission stalwart •

So far as can be known, Andries Pretorius was born around 1775 on the upper reaches of the Great Fish River. In 1805 he, his wife Martha, and several children left a frontier farm and gained admission to the LMS mission of Bethelsdorp, near Uitenhage in the eastern Cape. He was baptised in the Gariep in 1813 while assisting the Rev. John Campbell on his first tour of southern Africa.

Pretorius identified himself as a Bushman, exclaiming: 'Have not I, a Bushman, found grace! Was not I taken from the muzzle of a gun, and made an heir of eternal life?'

Pretorius was active in the economic life of Bethelsdorp. He seems to have been self-employed as a sawyer and trader who was able, with the wagon and oxen he acquired, to profit from the timber trade and transport business. He had a keen sense of grievance concerning the mistreatment of Khoesaan servants by the colonists, appearing prominently among the witnesses to charges which the missionaries laid before the Cape government. One response to this campaign was the initiation of a circuit court to hear complaints in the outlying districts of the colony. Despite the fact that these activities were unpopular with most officials, Pretorius's reputation was such that he was called upon to lead 'loyal' Khoesaan in the colony's defence.

In 1814, Pretorius became a deacon at Bethelsdorp and his wife became a deaconess. He regularly assisted in the founding of new stations: the Xhosa mission on the Kat River in 1815; the Tswana mission at 'New Lattakoo' (Kuruman); the Bushman missions at Ramah and Konnah, outstations of Griquatown. His friendship with the missionary James Read survived Read's adultery with his young daughter, Sabina. Although Read acknowledged paternity, Sabina's child was baptised Isaac Johannes Pretorius.

Pretorius headed a party which moved to the 'Hottentot' buffer zone known as the Kat River Settlement. Soon after the frontier war of 1834–5 broke out, his erf was requisitioned

for a military camp (afterwards Fort Armstrong). He was allocated a new erf in a section called the Balfour Commonage. His son Andries, who had an erf in Readsdale Commonage, became a veldcornet. They and others of his family were active in Settlement affairs. There are good reasons to suppose that Andries jun. is the veldcornet 'of Bushman origin' who proposed that their church extend a helping hand to 'the remnant of his father's nation' known to be nearby. Their search led them to Madolo, some 90 km to the north.

The next frontier war (the 'War of the Axe') was a severe setback to the Kat River Settlement. In its wake, Pretorius with several family members moved across the Gariep to Philippolis, a Griqua (formerly Bushman) mission. In 1853 he bought 'Meyers Kraal', a farm belonging to the Griqua chief, Adam Kok III. While Griqua-owned farms were passing to European owners at an increasing rate, a Bushman buyer had no need to fear exclusion at that stage. Pretorius was still away when another frontier war broke out (the eighth) and some Kat River residents rebelled against their government.

The government's response was to confiscate the property of rebels, and of those absent from the Settlement. Pretorius and several of his sons found out that their erven had been sold to white colonists. This was in accord with a decision to 'break up the Hottentot *exclusive* settlement'. Its founder, Stockenström, who represented the eastern districts in the Cape's new Legislative Council, took up the cudgels on Pretorius's (and others') behalf.

When it was found that the confiscations were actually illegal, a Compensation Act was passed and a commission was set up to adjudicate the numerous claims. Pretorius and three of his sons, Andries, Jan and Maurits, returned to support their claims when the adjudication took place at Balfour in March 1858. Pretorius died the next month, while still in the Settlement.

18 • Madolo: A Bushman chief's mission experiment •

Madolo (born c.1789) is said by the ethnologist George Stow to have lived as a young man in a large cave near present-day Whittlesea. Stow, who visited the region in 1867 when Madolo was no longer alive, was told that the LMS pioneer, Dr Van der Kemp, had visited him there. What is certain is that, in 1839, Madolo met the LMS missionary James Read, who was then working at Philipton in the Kat River Settlement. From a Bushman member of his congregation, Read had heard of 'wild' Bushmen living not far away. The party sent to find them came upon Madolo near the Black Kei River.

In September 1839, a place within Madolo's territory was found where he and his followers were encouraged to build houses, grow crops, and adopt European clothes. In 1840, Read's son Joseph established a chapel and a school there. The missionaries claimed that Madolo welcomed these changes, in preference to his former way of life when he, like 'the wild beasts', had no other occupation but to look for food.

This story may be true but, equally, it may reflect the missionaries' need to prove their 'civilising mission's' success. The hard reality which obliged the chief to become a crop farmer was that 'other persons were settling near him, and game was becoming scarce, and he feared it would soon fail'. Some of his people were converted but Madolo himself was never baptised.

Dr John Philip was favourably impressed when he visited the station in January 1842. From 15 Bushman families then, the community grew to around three hundred family heads, many of whom were Khoekhoen, Bastards and Bantu-speakers rather than Bushmen.

Madolo and New Bethelsdorp (as the station was named in 1844) attracted distinguished travellers from abroad. James Backhouse, a visiting Quaker, reported on it. Artist Thomas Baines described his April 1848 visit in waggish tones which made Madolo a figure of fun: Baines met a 'diminutive old man … [who] when we enquired for the Chief Madore, informed us that he was himself the bearer of that honourable distinction.'

New Bethelsdorp men helped to defend the Kat River Settlement during the frontier war known as the War of the Axe (1846–7). These colonial levies – around 200 strong – received rations but no pay for months at a time. After the war the Governor, Sir Harry Smith, annexed vast areas to the colony. Loyal chiefs like Madolo hoped that they would be rewarded with land.

Smith undertook to recognise Madolo's claim to land, an area some 80 km by 40 km. But other allies in the recent war, for example the Mfengu ('Fingoes'), had been promised land. Local officials earmarked portions of Madolo's territory for them. In 1849 it was proposed to levy a £1 quitrent in the new district where the Bushman station lay. After meeting Madolo that year, the Rev. J.J. Freeman campaigned against the quitrent. He foresaw that the station (renamed Freemanton in his honour) would be destroyed by unchecked encroachment and other fraudulent means.

Colonial policy proved detrimental in other ways. The Cape official Sir Walter Stanford describes an incident where a chief named Ndhlela complained to a colonial official about the Bushmen and was advised 'that he and the Bushmen must settle their own affairs. This Ndhlela promptly took to be sufficient authority for him to attack Madolo, and he did so with such vigour that the Bushmen, notwithstanding a brave resistance, were scattered far and wide.' Madolo and some of his followers fled to caves on the far bank of the White Kei.

When Stow visited the area he heard that Madolo and 'the shattered wreck of his once powerful tribe' had retreated yet again before he died in about 1860 and had sought refuge in the Drakensberg.

pursued by them, equally as by the boors, with the utmost animosity'.

The weight of evidence in the historical record supports the view that Bushmen were likely to be seen as adversaries and the rightful prey of white and Bastard pastoralists. Episodes of clientage, which the protagonists arranged among themselves, and periods of coexistence which government or sympathetic parties managed and encouraged, were exceptions to this pattern of relations on the Cape's frontier.

The missionaries and the Bushmen

After Kicherer left Happy Prospect Fountain (Blyvooruitzichts Fontein), founded in 1799, and the Zak River mission (1800–5), the LMS waited almost a decade to found another mission to the Bushmen. This station, known as Toornberg (now Colesberg), and another, called Hephzibah, closed after a few years. The reasons for these closures had to do with isolation, poor resourcing by the parent society, the attitudes among the various parties involved and the qualities of individuals in charge. Collins believed that 'the happiest effects were felt during the continuance of [Kicherer's] institution, which was abandoned from no cause but pecuniary difficulties'. By contrast, Stockenström averred that Toornberg 'failed through the conduct of its head'. Although new stations were established north and south of the Gariep, they also languished from lack of support and other causes.

Stockenström felt that a 'tract of country' north of the Gariep should be set aside where missionaries could protect, rather than preach to, the Bushmen. Only when they had been 'raised', from hunter-gatherers to 'graziers', would it be 'time to lead them to higher improvements'. This idea was unlikely to appeal to missionaries, who attached great importance to bringing people they saw as heathen to the Christian God.

A few Bushmen joined missions which catered mainly for the Khoekhoen. Andries Pretorius, the patriarch of an important London Missionary Society family, was one (see Box 17).

By the mid-1800s, Bushmen were to be found only in scattered pockets within the colony. To the east a few bands retained their independence beyond the border and in the Drakensberg. The Bushman chief Madolo (see Box 18) was one of these. His story and that of Andries Pretorius illustrate the pressures on eastern Bushmen and the outcome of the mission option which, in different circumstances, both men chose.

Bushmen and colonial law

William Somerville, a Cape official during the first British occupation, believed that at first Bushmen had brought back the Europeans' livestock when it strayed. Later, when the farmers started to insist that they 'should find the strayed cattle, and to punish them for the theft' whenever they failed, they ceased being honest and the spiral of violence began.

Claims such as this, equally with claims that Bushmen were inveterate thieves, should make us ask for evidence which explains the conflict attributed to theft which spanned more than two centuries.

After visiting the eastern districts, Somerville urged 'lenient treatment to conciliate [Bushman] affections'. He cited the example of J.P. van der Walt of Tarka whom he had met in 1799; Van der Walt's servants, some seventy Bushmen who lived on his farm, were entirely trustworthy and faithful due to the kind treatment they received.

The Bushman policies which Governor Macartney introduced in 1797 (and Somerville approved) were a departure from the policies which had characterised the 1700s, although the Van der Walt example shows that certain colonists were trying out new methods on their own. But if in some ways more humane, the British resembled the early settlers in wishing to make servants of the Bushmen. As the two Stockenströms explained, once the 'wild Bushmen' had been 'tamed' they became useful servants and were indistinguishable from 'Hottentots'.

This transformation was, however, likely to be slow. In 1809 Collins advised that 'it will be a considerable time before the plan of engaging the Bosjesmen to serve the inhabitants during registered periods can be conveniently adopted'. For this reason, Bushmen were not covered by the proclamation issued that same year (1 November 1809) which imposed passes and controlled the labour of 'Hottentots'. In reality, of course, Bushmen were becoming 'Hottentots' throughout

19 • How some Bushman child apprentices
were detained by farmers •

In February 1829, T.Y. van Buuren of Somerset District complained about a 'Bushman' servant, Doortje, whom he sent away when, he claimed, she pretended illness. When Doortje returned 'only to fetch [her] child', he tried to make her stay. She then used 'the most abusive language, cursing, swearing, and said she, "be d...md if I'll ever come to you again" … uttering the most violent and horrible words imaginable, venting her fury with belching out the most railing expressions, jumping and running to and fro like a spring buck; that at last I was obliged to send to the Gaoler, with request to put her in the Tronk.'

Van Buuren asked the magistrate to order Doortje 'home' to work for him again: 'Convinced that you will not permit that the here mentioned oppressed Family [his own]

will be abused by a Boshiesmans woman nor by anybody else.' Without Doortje he was obliged to mind his flock himself.

A farmer, George Devenish, told a similar tale concerning Els (said to be a 'Hottentot'), who returned to claim her children. Devenish wished to detain the older ones who were, he said, 'of much use to me'. In the course of their tug-of-war Els flew into such a 'passion' that he had to 'tie her to a waggon' to calm her down. Devenish also complained that his 'Busch Boy Slinger', apprenticed to him for fourteen years in 1817, was 'impertinent' and threatening to leave. As a Cape proclamation of 1817 limited apprenticeship to ten years, and the incident occurred in 1829, it seems that Devenish was in the wrong. Ten months later Slinger still complained that he was not allowed to leave.

the proclamation's life. In 1828 it was replaced by Ordinance 50, which gave 'Hottentots and other free persons of colour', including Bushmen, equality before the law (see *The Cape Herders*).

A proclamation of 1817 also attempted to regulate child apprenticeship. Some officials were concerned that children captured by commandos and given to the farmers were, in the words of the historian J.S. Marais, 'held in virtual slavery'. The proclamation applied as well to any children whom Bushman workers left behind on the farms while they themselves were away, or who were brought by parents to be cared for during times of hunger (which occurred more frequently as Bushman hunting grounds were swallowed up by farms). Despite the 1817 law, child labour was easily abused on the frontier.

By the 1820s 'Hottentot' no longer meant a person practising a pastoral way of life. It referred to those Khoesan who were absorbed into the Cape economy. 'Bushmen', on the other hand, although they might have experienced life at mission stations or on farms, lived for the most part 'in the

wild'. Soon after Ordinance 50 became law, a frontier official complained about 'a Band of runaway Bushmen and Hottentots' – but corrected himself: 'It does not appear that there are any Bushmen *properly so-called* among them but that they are wholly composed of Persons who have run away from the Farmers with whom they have been in service' (emphasis added).

Bushman bandits in the colony, Bushman bands along the boundary

The commando system did not stop when the thirty-year war (1770–1800) came to an end but was a feature of frontier life in the 1800s. The colonists continued to be fearful that the Bushmen might 'get the upper hand of us'.

In September 1828, in the district of Somerset, one of the runaways (complained of above) injured a farmer with a poisoned arrow. The farmer heard the 'banditti' shout: 'We do not mean to quit this place; you may come back tomorrow and you will receive the same reception you received today.' Their defiance brought to a head the colonists' anger about livestock theft, and the maiming and killing of breeding stock. An armed patrol entered deep bush near the Mancazana River and captured alive five men, five women and eight children. The male captives – who were well known as they had worked on farms, or been in jail, or both – were sent to prison by the circuit court. The injured farmer had survived the poisoned arrow, or one at least among them would have been hanged for murder.

A year later the field commandant of Beaufort District warned that Bushmen, thought to be 400-strong, threatened 'een inval op die Colonie' [an invasion of the Colony]. The Governor, Sir Lowry Cole, authorised a commando to disperse this band, who had 'struck such terror in the minds of the Inhabitants' that families fled from 44 farms and came together for their self-defence. One night, the Bushmen surrounded the sleeping laager and fired into the camp. The next day 66 arrows were picked up. A hundred burghers were called out and the crisis passed. Bushman survivors probably retreated over the Gariep.

The conflict moved with the frontier, to the north and east. In 1847 a Natal patrol caught up with Bushmen who were driving off a farmer's herd, whereupon, according to John Wright, 'the thieves ran among the cattle and began stabbing them'. The Bushmen identified correctly the threats to their way of life but gained only temporary relief by the responses which seemed possible to them.

Even when the colonists seemed to be in opposing camps, there was an underlying unity of view. Following a theft by Bushmen, the noted humanitarian, Thomas Pringle, exclaimed: 'ungrateful

6.8: *This drawing, which appeared in* Die Burger *in 1971, bore the caption: 'Naas die Bybel was die voorlaaier die Trekboer se kosbaarste besitting. Dit was sy enigste beskerming teen die Boesmans en roofdiere.' (Next to the Bible the muzzle-loader was the* trekboer's *most precious possession. It was his only protection against the Bushmen and predators.)*

schelms! Even after I have celebrated them in song' (see Pringle's poem, page 34). Though he abhorred the cruelties inflicted on the Bushmen by the Dutch he believed that 'however guilty the colony may have been in pursuing a system of injustice and oppression which had ... driven most of these unhappy outlaws to their present mode of life, it was obvious that their predatory career could not be allowed to continue.' The commando which Pringle called out was not different from commandos which had hunted Bushmen in the past.

CHAPTER SEVEN

Surviving against the odds

After Ordinance 50 of 1828, the Bushmen of the Cape Colony were subject to the laws applying to free persons (that is, people who were not slaves). Bushmen beyond the borders were treated as foreigners. They could gain legal entry only by signing a labour contract with a colonist. By mid-century, many of these Bushmen were incorporated in the new British colony of Natal and the two Afrikaner statelets, the Orange Free State and the South African Republic.

Living beyond the colony

Some 'tame' Bushmen (on the way to being 'Hottentots') trekked from the Cape with the colonists who employed them. The Bushman servants of pioneer trekker Louis Trichardt – among them Keyser, Wintervogel, Ragel and Koot – left the Cape in 1835, and some survived to reach Lourenço Marques (Maputo) in 1838.

Faced with the loss of hunting grounds and a life of servitude on the farms, other colonial Bushmen joined those who were long established beyond the Gariep. There too they struggled to survive among land-hungry Griqua and the European graziers whose periodic use of pastures turned to full-scale settlement in ever greater numbers.

The cycle of theft and reprisal continued in 'Transorangia'. An official wrote: 'It is certainly much to be regretted that this unfortunate Race should continue to lead such a life as they have hitherto done by which means bloodshed is so often the result.'

'Peaceable Bushmen' who lived with the missionaries were harassed by *trekboers* who resented the fact that they were unavailable as herdsmen, although the missionaries claimed that 'the Boors had got almost all the children in their possession before we came here'.

In 1846 Adam Kok III introduced a 'Bushman Act' requiring Bushmen who were not with the missionaries to enter into contracts with the Griqua or European farmers in his domain. Violence occurred at many sites. In 1850 the artist Thomas Baines heard about 'five Bushmen hanged at Bloem Fontein for the murder of a whole family of white people'.

On the Natal side of the Drakensberg, the situation was fluid until the 1870s when 'the Bushman problem' was effectively controlled. The historian John Wright has identified three main periods of Bushman raiding in Natal, between 1845 and 1872, with some 64 raids recorded during that time.

During the 1850s a gang of about a hundred men known as the 'Thola', which was said to consist of Bushmen and 'coloureds' under a Bushman chief, operated near the headwaters of the Mzimvubu in the Drakensberg. The Natal authorities tried to stop British traders from exchanging guns with the gang for stolen goods, such as horses. Wright speculates that Dick King, famous as the 'Saviour of Natal' after his epic ride to Grahamstown in 1842, was one of these.

A proclamation of 1866 placing 'a total ban ... on the hunting of eland and hartebeest, together with certain birds' and closed seasons for other animals, owing to the shooting out of game, impacted on Bushmen as well as on the more destructive colonists. Wright observes: 'Nowhere in these early years is there a single record of a voice being raised in their defence.' After 1872 there are few references to independent Bushmen in the records of Natal.

20

• Bushmen sentenced to transportation to the Australian colonies •

The Cape was included in the British system of convict transportation to New South Wales and Van Diemen's Land (Tasmania). Transportation was a form of banishment from places where the convicts had committed their crimes.

In 1834, twenty Bushmen were arrested for attacking a Winterveld farm. All were condemned to death when they were tried for murder, housebreaking and robbery. Afterwards, the judge observed that 'Public justice ... would shrink ... from executing Capital punishment upon so large a number of Delinquents'.

Four were hanged, and the judge commuted the other sixteen sentences to transportation. But when Governor D'Urban tried to send the men to New South Wales in 1836, he was prevented from 'a step so much to be deprecated with reference to the interests of that Colony'. It appears that the British government, which had already sent many blacks from the West Indies and other colonies, intended in future to transport white offenders only to Australia.

In 1838 some soldiers of the Cape Mounted Riflemen, a 'Hottentot' and 'Bastard' regiment, shot and killed an officer. The mutineers were court-martialled and sentenced to death. Again, most of the sentences were commuted to transportation. In this case – since military discipline in British line regiments was uniform, regardless of race – the sentences were carried out. In 1840 the men were taken in the *Pekoe* to New South Wales.

There is good reason to think that some of the mutineers were members of the 'Bushman Company' of the CMR. Hendrik Uithaalder was 28 years old, married, illiterate, and around 1,4m tall (it was said he could neither saddle nor mount a horse without help). In accordance with the practice whereby convicts policed other convicts, Uithaalder and another CMR deserter named Stuurman Jantjes were sent to Moreton Bay (Brisbane) with the Border Police. This unit chased runaways, traced stray horses, escorted prisoners, kept the Aborigines at bay, carried letters and so forth. Uithaalder got into trouble again, was transferred to Van Diemen's Land and, after yet another criminal offence, was hanged in 1863.

Bushmanland and war along the Gariep

In the mid-1800s the Cape colonists found that the semi-desert of the northern Cape, which few had coveted before, was suited to merino sheep. In consequence violence escalated in the region in line with well-established patterns: hundreds of Bushmen were killed and the survivors turned to banditry.

The government appointed a magistrate, Louis Anthing, to investigate. His 1863 report provided much detail about the conflict, and practical proposals for restoring peace. This document shows how Anthing tried to break from the destructive patterns of the past in an effort to restore peace.

Anthing wrote this report after his return to Cape Town where he brought three prisoners as well as Herklaas, the father of one of the youths (said to be 11 or 12 years old) who had killed a Bastard farmer's grandsons. The government ignored his proposals and the press branded him as partial to the Bushmen. Not long after, he was transferred to another post.

Fifteen years later, at a time of severe drought, a war broke out along the Gariep in which Bushmen and Korana opposed the Bastard and European colonists. It was reported that 'the Bushmen and Koranas [boast] that they will not leave their depredations until they have succeeded in retaking

21

• Excerpts from Louis Anthing's report on the northern Cape •

Cape Town, 21st April, 1863

'Sir, – I have the honour to submit herewith a report of my proceedings in connection with the service in which I have been for some time engaged ... On the 22nd of June I received a note from a coloured farmer, who was squatting about fifteen miles from our post, informing me that his two grandsons had been killed by Bushmen ... I found [the bodies] pierced with arrows ... the fact of the cattle [they were watching] having been left untouched appeared to me to indicate a state of things from which more mischief might be expected ... My first step was to call together a number of armed men (coloured and European farmers), and with these and some constables I went to arrest the murderers of the two young men ... After some fruitless search, however, I dismissed the commando, perceiving unmistakable indications of an intention on their part to thwart my plans for inducing the Bushmen to surrender, and to massacre the whole party whenever they should be fallen in with. I was determined to endeavour to avoid such a catastrophe. After the dismissal of the commando, I employed

certain Bushmen with whom I had become acquainted, and desired them to use their influence to bring the hostile band to reason, and to arrest the two of their number charged with the murders. This was eventually effected, and I took the two prisoners into custody at Kenhart. The band, upon the assurance that I had been sent to do justice to all, dispersed, relinquishing all plans of further hostilities ... The Bushmen are now all quiet ... I believe that many of them will undergo a great extent of suffering before they will again touch the flocks of the farmers ... But hunger is a terrible prompter ... I would again venture to repeat the recommendation, which I have already submitted, namely,

1. To locate the Bush-people on certain places to be set apart for that purpose in the lands which their tribes have for many generations occupied.
2. To sell so much of these lands as may be sufficient to provide for the purchase of stock and some other necessaries for their future support ... I estimate the total number of the Bush-people at five hundred souls ...

that part of the Colony which extends from the Bokkeveld to the Orange River'.

A stream of prisoners arrived in Cape Town from the northern Cape. Some who took part in the war were convicted as rebels and sent to Robben Island. Those convicted of lesser offences, such as stock theft, served their sentences in the Breakwater Prison. Some wives and children, who would have starved if left behind, came too.

The Bushmen speak

Now and then a European's opinion of Bushmen went against the common view. Burchell had been 'led to expect only a set of beings without reason

or intellect'. Instead, 'the first individuals of this nation, whom we fell in with, were men of lively manners and shrewd understandings'.

Andrew Smith traced the worsening hostilities between the Bushmen and settlers, from theft to murder-and-theft, and concluded 'that these were people not devoid of intellect but, on the contrary, extremely acute observers and fully competent to turn their observations to good account. Here methinks I hear it whispered ... their actions are the mere impulses of natural cunning. If there are those who will venture such an opinion, let them repair to the haunts of the savage, listen to his orations and his reason for what he may propose, and observe how he regulates his

7.1: *Some Bushman prisoners at the Breakwater Prison in Cape Town in the late 1800s.*

7.2: *An interior view of the Breakwater Prison.*

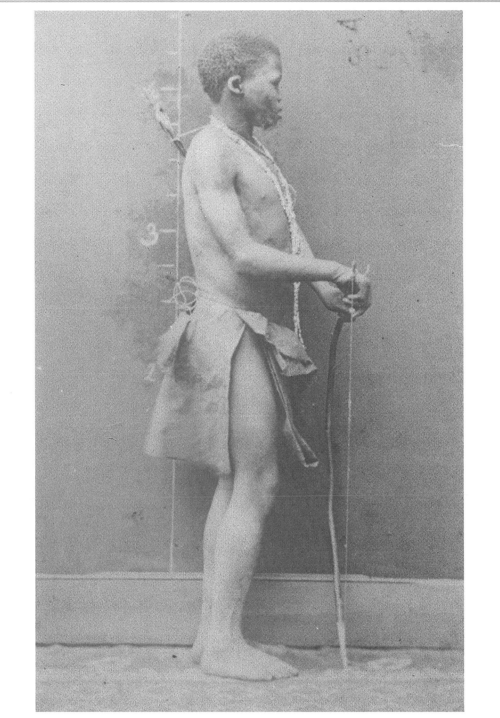

7.3: *Some of the Bushman prisoners, and others like Tuma (!Uma) shown here, who was sent down specially from Namibia, were studied by Wilhelm Bleek and his assistants to record their physical characteristics, language, folklore and way of life. While dressed Bushman-style, Tuma was measured.*

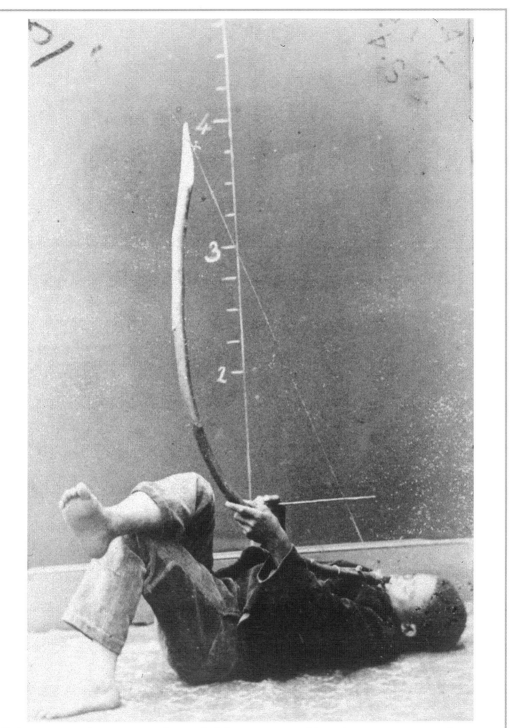

7.4: *In European dress, Tuma was photographed playing on a musical bow. Most instruments were ordinary hunting bows, although some players made special bows on which to perform. Perhaps Tuma was asked to demonstrate this way of performing, while lying on his back, as it is more usual to sit or squat.*

actions in conformity to his reasons, and they will probably return fraught with admiration of his intelligence and with regrets at its not being directed to better purposes.'

Though many meetings were reported, few Europeans recorded Bushman speech, apart from the examples of defiance which have been mentioned.

Somerville was an exception in being sensitive to other moods. 'Of the Bushmen', he wrote, 'it is to be observed that they are much more cheerful and talkative than most other Hottentots – the certainty of a hearty meal never fails to inspire conversation and set them laughing ...' In a context where Britons like himself, who were new to the Cape, were quick to denigrate the Dutch, he observed: 'They have many jokes against the boors about their courage and other subjects – and near

Snewberg and Tarka where the Bushman [sic] amuse themselves by drawing upon the Rocks, the figure of a Boor with his long Gun and large Hat is frequently to be seen. They sometimes adorn him with a long tail also ...' As a postscript he suggested that painting might be a dying art: 'None of the Bushmen hereabouts are at all acquainted with drawing.'

In 1808 the Moravian missionary J.A. Kuster interviewed the convert Jacob Adams, said to be the only Bushman at Genadendal, who was around 100 years of age. Kuster worked through an interpreter and the evidence he took appears to paraphrase (and probably condense) Adams's speech. This witness, who said his father was a 'Bosjeman' king, rejected the savagery of his early life and explained how it had come about: 'Formerly they, as well as all the other Hottentot tribes, were a

---

22 • //Kabbo (Oud Jantje Tooren) tells of his arrest in 1869 •

'The [constable] took me; he bound my arms ... We were in jail. We put our legs into the stocks. The Korannas came to us, when our legs were in the stocks ... we ate sheep on the way ... to Victoria [West]; our wives ate their sheep on the way, as they came to Victoria. We came to roll stones at Victoria, while we worked at the road ... We again had our arms bound to the wagon chain; we walked along, while we were fastened to the wagon chain, as we came to Beaufort [West] ... We came into Beaufort jail ... We walked upon the road ... We walked, following the wagon, being bound ... until we came to the Breakwater ... A white man took us to meet the train in the night ... the train ran, bringing us to the Cape. We came into the Cape prison house when we were tired, we and the Korannas; we lay down to sleep at noon.'

7.5: //Kabbo, whose name means 'Dream', was the most effective story-teller among the /Xam informants. He told Wilhelm Bleek that a story 'is like the wind, it comes from a far-off quarter, and we feel it.'

7.6: *!Kweiten ta //ken (Griet / Rachel), wife of ≠Kasin (Klaas Katkop), with one of their children. !Kweiten ta //ken was the most important informant from whom the Bleeks heard a woman's perspective on Bushman lifeways. She was with them for a few months during 1874–5.*

quiet and well-disposed people, but being deprived of their land, and robbed of their cattle by the Europeans, they became, in their turn, savage, and given to plunder.' According to this account, 'The Missionary wished to hear more of the singular customs of the Bosjemans, but Jacob Adams desired his interpreter to tell him that he did not like to remember and relate such bad things, having at his baptism renounced the devil and all his works, and therefore wished to have nothing more to do with his old customs.' While the Moravian archive is immensely valuable respecting those called 'Hottentots', Adams's is a lonely Bushman voice.

A treasure trove of Bushman folklore and life narratives was created in the 1870s through the collaboration of Cape (/Xam) Bushmen and the family of a German-born language specialist, Wilhelm Bleek. Among the /Xam informants, six stood out: /A!kunta, //Kabbo, /Han≠kass'o, Diä!kwain, !Kweiten ta //ken (the only woman) and ≠Kasin. Many of the informants had served prison terms for crimes ranging from culpable homicide to theft.

While interviews were carried out, they lived with the Bleeks, often for many months, in the Cape Town suburb of Mowbray. After Bleek's death in 1875, his sister-in-law, Lucy Lloyd, and daughters, especially Dorothea Bleek, devoted many years to completing the work. Over 11 000 pages of script resulted from their interviews and field trips to the northern Cape.

Bushmen and history: If you're not in the book, do you exist?

Under the heading 'Bushman relations with the Bastards and the European colonists', we referred to a debate which asks if peace was not more dangerous to Bushman survival than ceaseless war, even though warfare was costly to them in loss of life. Historians have noted that, in both the Sneeuwberg and the Roggeveld, Bushman resisters suffered many losses, yet managed to arrest *trek-boer* expansion for several decades. Their ferocity was recorded by the Dutch officer R.J. Gordon, who wrote that when cornered all were likely to be 'shot as they will take no quarter but defend themselves with the most stubborn courage to the last'.

In 1834 Dr Andrew Smith remarked: 'Flight … the Bushman regards as one of the most disgraceful acts of which man can be guilty.' Smith wondered if their suicidal stance was sheer bravery or was due, perhaps, to their abhorrence of the 'slavery' which awaited them if they were captured.

Nigel Penn explains the Bushmen's ultimate defeat, in regions which the colonists wanted, not simply as the result of the colonists' superior military strength. He suggests that the Bushman world-view – which looked to dreams, trance and the spirit world as sources of power – 'was no match' for the 'focused drive of the Europeans' in which 'power derived from material gain'. Beyond that, he considers the colonists' attempts to pacify the Bushmen by giving them stock, planting missionaries in their midst and encouraging their induction to farm life by waiving the labour contracts which were enforced on the Khoekhoen. Penn concludes: 'Time would unfold the paradoxical truth that peace could be as dangerous as war as far as the San were concerned …'

The 1800s saw the end of Bushman independence in much of southern Africa. The newcomers forgot that Bushmen had once inhabited the whole of the subcontinent and many thought that the survivors were a 'dying race'. The history books began to leave them out, or mention them only as ancient enemies. These perceptions have been proved false. Modern Bushmen are today fighting for their rights and for the recognition of their history, their culture and their land.

CHAPTER EIGHT

An ethnography of modern Bushmen

While the Bushman populations south of the Gariep River are known primarily through the archaeological and ethnohistorical record, the Bushmen of the Kalahari have been visited by anthropologists throughout the twentieth century. They have conducted ethnographic research and collected first-hand data on the social organisation and culture of contemporary Bushman peoples.

The early ethnographers, missionaries, colonial officers, surveyors and farmers were mostly German, Portuguese or English, working in the colonial territories of Angola, South West Africa (Namibia) and Bechuanaland (Botswana). They produced the first accounts of the Bushman population of the colonies. They – and more recent ethnographers such as Lorna Marshall and her family, and Richard Lee and others associated with the 'Harvard group' – have, for the most part, studied the !Kung. Lorna Marshall worked among the Ju/'hoansi of the Nyae Nyae–Dobe region of north-eastern Namibia and Richard Lee in north-western Botswana.

If some of the descriptions in this section resemble those found in the archaeological and historical record, it is because present-day life is similar to what we can reconstruct of the past.

Bushman populations

The basis for this account of Bushman society is Ju/'hoan society, which falls into the pattern anthropologists have called the 'foraging band society'. However, there are many other linguistic and ethnic groupings amongst the 105 000 or so Bushmen living in the various countries of southern Africa, and their ecological, economic and

23 • Population numbers of contemporary Bushmen, by country •

Botswana	49 475
Namibia	38 275
Angola	9 750
South Africa	4 700
Zambia	1 600
Zimbabwe	1 275

social organisation are not the same as the ones described here.

Because there is so much anthropological literature about the !Kung, it is commonly thought that they are representative of all Bushmen; that they *are* the Bushmen. This view does not, however, allow for the wide range of cultural variation found both within a particular region and across the whole of southern Africa.

Some of these regional differences may be explained by the volume, variety and distribution of rainfall, water holes, game, plants and plant communities in various areas of the same region. Other reasons for diversity, apart from ecological variation, are the particular historical circumstances of Bushmen in different regions. The most consequential of these involved contact with agro-pastoral groups who entered various parts of southern Africa at separate times and with various degrees of impact on the indigenous Bushman populations.

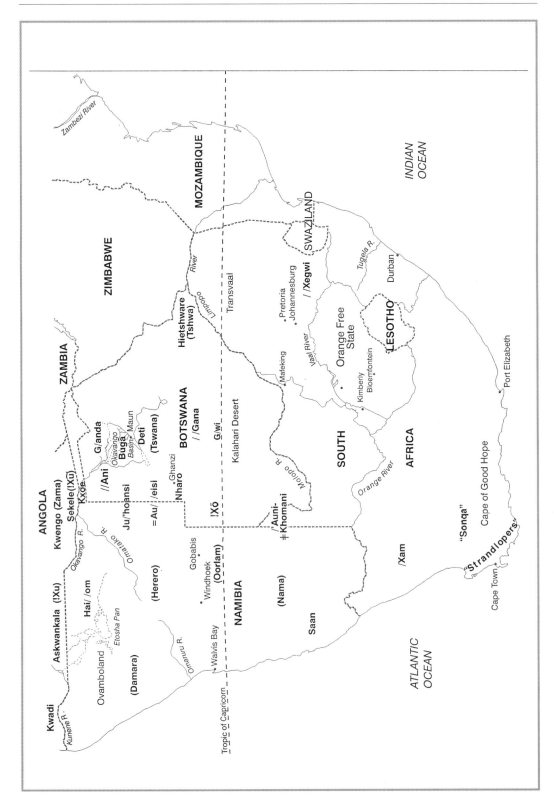

Cultural and social diversity of Bushmen

The accompanying map shows the extent of the linguistic and cultural diversity of the Bushmen. They speak nearly eighty dialects, and their languages fall into at least three mutually unintelligible families, subfamilies or groups. One of these, 'Khoe' or 'Central Khoesaan', includes such Khoekhoe languages as Hai//om, Nama, Griqua and !Ora (Korana).

The foraging band is the socio-economic organisation primarily of those Bushmen living in the more central, isolated and arid stretches of the Kalahari from the Central Kalahari Game Reserve up to the Dobe–Nyae Nyae area. Before tracing regional diversity among recent and contemporary Bushmen we should note that in the same region there is evidence of diversity as well over time. In the recent past, for example, there was much more game in most of the Kalahari regions where we now find foraging bands. In Ghanzi in the early 1800s herds were vast and included buffalo, elephant and rhinoceros. According to oral and ethnohistorical information, there was a greater emphasis on big-game hunting in those days. For example, pit traps were used in the past but they

have not been used by more recent Bushmen. In addition, the plant component in the subsistence economy of the Nharo and ≠Au//eisi was probably less significant than it is today, and the economic and political role of 'man the hunter' was then seemingly more important than that of 'woman the gatherer'.

North, east and west of these regions, towards the fringes of the Kalahari and in better-watered regions, live Bushman groups who augment their subsistence lifestyle with fishing or herding and cultivating. While fishing is a supplementary subsistence pattern for the hunting-gathering Kxoe of north-eastern Namibia, it is a primary subsistence pattern among the 'River Bushmen', the Bugakhoe and //Anikhoe of the Okavango and the Deti, eastern //Gana and Tyua (Chwa) living along the Boteti and Nata rivers of central and eastern Botswana.

Like the early coastal 'Cape Bushmen', these fisher-hunter-gatherers employ an elaborate technology that requires a greater amount of labour and organisation than simple hunting-gathering. They make stone dams, nets, fish baskets, dugouts and barbed spears. The Boteti River is exploited for more than its fish resources by the Bushmen living alongside it. They practised agriculture, taking advantage of the fertile flood plain produced by

8.1: *A D'Kar farm Bushwoman gathering khutsus (the 'Kalahari truffle') in 1995.*

the river. Some of the Boteti and Nata people also keep cattle and goats. The socio-political organisation resulting from such an economic base is quite different from the 'classic' Ju/'hoan-style foraging band.

Some of the Boteti and Nata Bushmen live in sedentary, markedly 'territorial' villages. Greater permanence enables them to store resources such as water. A stronger sense of 'ownership' has given rise to hereditary headmen who hold wide-ranging positions of authority: this enabled them to organise regional ritual activities and large-scale hunts and warfare. Short-distance trade by full-time traders, who bartered for goods by direct exchange, replaced the delayed, long-distance, non-mercantile trade of Kalahari Bushmen like the Ju/'hoansi (see Box 24).

On the western fringe of the Kalahari, in southern Angola and northern Namibia, are the agro-pastoral Bushman people, the Kwadi, Zama (or Kwengo), Sekele and !O!kung (!O!xu), who share similar socio-political features. The Angolan Kwengo, for instance, had hereditary chiefs owning up to forty head of cattle. Their subjects paid them tribute and the group lived in permanent, palisaded villages.

All the Bushman groupings living in these fringe areas of the Kalahari coexist with herding and agricultural peoples such as the Ovambo, Herero, Mbukushu, Kalanga and Tswana, and have done so for a long time. The relationship of Bushmen to their Bantu-speaking neighbours has been one of dependency, as slaves, serfs or servants to the herders. Black farmers tended to view the Bushmen as their social inferiors, and often treated them harshly, leaving a legacy of mutual hostility and wariness that continues to this day. However, the Bushmen also adopted many of the social attributes of their masters: clan organisation, polygyny, totemism, circumcision, witchcraft and sorcery beliefs. The most likely source for such patterns is the culture of the herders, as none is found in the society and culture of the Kalahari Bushmen.

Another herding people into whose economic, social and cultural orbit some Bushmen were drawn are the Nama; indeed some Bushmen have come to adopt the Nama language. In the 1800s the !Kung-speaking ≠Au//eisi and the Nharo of eastern Namibia were the serfs of the Oorlam

Nama settled around Gobabis. The Nama-speaking 'Namib Bushmen' of south-central Namibia occasionally worked at the cattle camps of the Nama and Basters. It is possible that they were, in fact, impoverished Nama, driven into arid lands unsuited for cattle.

The Hai//om derived their language from the Nama, along with certain political and ritual traits, such as inherited chiefship and female initiation practices. From the Damara, who were their servants, they drew the cosmological trait of the 'holy fire', the ritual attitude to the main camp fire, connoting peace and solidarity, while the Herero may have been the source of the feature of matrilineal descent. In the 1800s the Hai//om mined copper and salt, which they traded with their Bantu-speaking neighbours for ceramic vessels and iron.

The Hai//om are an example of how the Bushmen 'forage for ideas'. They show an openness to other cultures and a readiness to adopt outside customs and practices. This is another reason for the marked cultural diversity of these people.

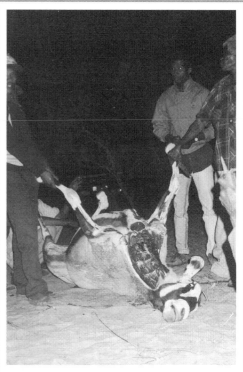

8.2: *Skinning a gemsbok at Ghanzi, 1995.*

8.3: *The farm Bushwoman !Ani with gathered roots (/'kaba).*

Bushmen of the Kalahari

Until recently the Bushmen of the Kalahari lived as hunter-gatherers in societies based, more or less, on the foraging band so well known from the Ju/'hoansi !Kung. Other Kalahari groups include the ≠Au//eisi and Nharo of the Ghanzi district, the G/wi (/Gui) and western //Gana of the central Kalahari Game Reserve, and the !Kõ (!Xõ) and /'Auni-≠Khomani of the arid southern Kalahari, in south-eastern Botswana and the Northern Cape province of South Africa.

The Kalahari, an arid, sand-filled plain and bushveld traversed with dunes and dry river beds, is more hospitable than it looks for those people who know how to find its food resources and deal with its seasonal changes. The food resources are surprisingly rich; the principal uncertainty is the vital resource of water. Rainfall patterns are unpredictable and the annual rainfall of 350 mm may fluctuate widely by several hundred millimetres above or below that figure. Too much rain rots wild melons and brings mosquitoes and malaria to the water pans. This can be devastating, as was the case in the summer of 1997 when many people contracted malaria.

During the five-month summer rainy season from October to March, the rains may be unevenly distributed over a band territory (n!ore) or a range of neighbouring n!ores. Normally no rain whatsoever falls during the seven months of winter and people have to draw water from the few permanent water holes found in a n!ore or adjoining n!ores. In the really dry regions inhabited by some of the G/wi and !Kõ, the only sources of water are roots or the rumen and stomach contents of game animals.

During the rainy season plants and animals are relatively abundant. Most of the African savanna ungulates – wildebeest, hartebeest, gemsbok, eland – are found in the Kalahari. Some migrate seasonally to summer grazing areas; others, such as kudu, springbok and steenbok, are hunted all year round. Warthog, springhare, antbear, porcupine and, to a lesser extent, giraffe are also economically important. Species of birds that are taken include francolin, ducks and geese (in the summer) and ostrich. Ostrich eggs are used both for food, producing mega-omelettes, and for technological purposes. The unbroken eggshell makes an excellent container for storing and carrying water. Broken into fragments it is used to make beads. Reptiles (tortoises and snakes) and insects (termites and click beetles) are also a source of food, click beetles in particular being an important part of the diet of people such as the G/wi living in the more arid regions. The poison beetle *Diamphidia simplex* yields the deadly arrow poison, and the honey bee produces the Bushmen's greatest delicacy, apart from fat and meat.

Kalahari Bushmen utilise some fifty species of animals for food, about a third of them regularly, but their knowledge of animals extends also to non-hunted species such as predators and song birds. The Ju/'hoansi have names for 260 animals and the !Kõ, who are reported to have distinct names for almost all the mammals in their arid Kalahari stretches, can identify 77 different birds and 65 insects as well.

The Bushwomen's knowledge of plants is extensive. About a hundred species are gathered. Leading the list of staple plant foods are the calorie- and protein-rich *mongongo* nuts (*Ricinodendron rantanenii*) of the north-central Kalahari and the *mangetti* bean (*Bauhinia esculanta*) of the central Kalahari. Other plant foods include wild seeds, berries, fruit, onions, leaves, melons, truffles, tubers, roots and tree sap. Trees, many of them dead and dry, also provide firewood.

Subsistence patterns

As with hunting-gathering people in other parts of the world, the basic division of labour among the Bushmen is by gender: men are hunters and women gatherers, each accomplished in his or her subsistence role. Men are expert at animal identification and animal behaviour and can read tracks with uncanny accuracy. Women are superb field botanists. They can identify plants individually – in some instances by only a tiny bit of vine or foliage low on the ground indicating a large root or tuber below the surface – and also in terms of clusters or plant communities. This knowledge is shared, so that men are also able to gather plants to provide for themselves during a protracted men-only hunting expedition. Women and youths set snares for small animals and will bag tortoises, birds and insects when out on gathering trips. The pace of work at gathering and hunting is quite

24 • 'We don't trade with things, we trade with people' •

This was the explanation given by a somewhat exasperated Ju/'hoan informant to Richard Lee, after a lengthy discussion in which the anthropologist struggled to understand what, to a Westerner, was a very different exchange system from his own.

It is a system in which the goods exchanged are not an end in themselves, but a means to a wider, social end: to create and solidify bonds of friendship, which may also become bonds of mutual help.

Another expression of the social nature of this sort of exchange is that goods become gifts. The most common and desirable *xaro* partners are close blood relatives, but distant kin are also included. Polly Wiessner, who studied this pattern extensively in the 1970s, noted that *xaro* acted as a form of 'social insurance' through which risks emanating from an uncertain environment could be 'pooled' or spread out. She demonstrated how partnerships formed far-flung exchange networks, operating along circuitous pathways that could extend for hundreds of kilometres and involve dozens of bands and hundreds of individuals.

The Ju/'hoansi distinguish this type of exchange from direct exchange or barter, for which they have a different term (*//amakwe*). In barter, one item is exchanged for another, then and there, and the exchange of the goods, ideally at a profit, is its prime if not only purpose. In the socially motivated *xaro* exchange, the return gift is delayed, by weeks, months or even a year. By delaying the debt,

the bond of friendship and reciprocity or mutuality between partners is prolonged, as well as acknowledged and reinforced. If the delay is too long, however, or persistently reciprocated in an unbalanced fashion, tension may be created in the partnership.

The goods exchanged in *xaro* are non-food items of a wide variety. Virtually all items of material culture, including dogs, are suitable. According to Wiessner, about 70 per cent of a Ju/'hoan woman's household goods come from *xaro* partners. Especially favoured among male partners are arrows, spears and knives, while ostrich eggshell beadwork is women's favourite *xaro* gift. Also coveted as *xaro* items are objects from the outside; amongst present-day Ju/'hoansi and Ghanzi farm Bushmen these are articles of clothing, pots, enamel ware, flashlights or watches. In pre-colonial times this category of objects may have included pottery and iron implements and weapons manufactured by Bantu-speaking people. These goods may have reached even isolated Kalahari groups through *xaro* pathways, without any direct contact with the black producers of the exotic materials. Such long-distance movement of material goods is of interest to archaeologists working on Stone Age and Iron Age sites in the Kalahari like Cho/ana in the Sandveld of northern Namibia. It suggests that the presence of such objects may not necessarily signify direct contact between Bushmen and black traders.

relaxed and averages 2,4 days per person (about 20 hours) per week. The efficient and successful way in which they obtain food in the Kalahari has led some anthropologists to apply the term 'affluent' to their way of life!

Although hunters of one camp may bring in as

many as eighteen animals yielding some 230 kilograms in a month, hunters are not always successful. This means that plants gathered by women provide the stable and staple food component, rather than meat, and make up from 60 to 80 per cent of the people's diet. This contributes signifi-

25 • The Great Kalahari debate: Two visions of the Bushmen •

A current controversial issue in Kalahari studies, and in hunter-gatherer studies generally, is whether to regard the simple foraging and egalitarian society of the Bushmen as a distinct cultural type, or as a social pattern that resulted from the relationship of dependency existing for centuries between Bushmen and their agropastoral neighbours with more complex and stronger political systems.

The debate, which started in the early 1980s, has been quite heated, as it presents two radically opposed visions of the Bushmen and of societies like theirs. The one vision sees aboriginal people, more or less isolated, culturally autonomous and politically free. They follow a technologically simple, nomadic, foraging way of life in which everything is shared.

The newer 'revisionist' vision sees these same people as dominated by regional agropastoral state societies, occupying the lowest rung in the class system as servants and labourers. As part of their incorporation into the larger society, they have themselves adopted material traits (including the possession of stock animals) and social institutions and values that revolve around accumulation, power and hierarchy.

The one is a vision of independence and equality, and social and ecological harmony; the other of dependence, oppression and absorption by as well as adoption of patterns of inequality.

The isolationist approach rests on intensive, long-term fieldwork and is concerned primarily with how Bushmen use their culture to adapt to their arid environment. This is the theoretical approach of cultural ecology. Anthropologists working with it study such things as land-use strategies, patterns of mobility and distribution, population control mechanisms, division of labour, and alliance or network formations through sharing, kinship and marriage. They also study neighbours or settlers and the Bushmen's patterns of interaction with them, especially in trade and labour.

The revisionist approach, on the other hand, is based as much on historical (and some archaeological) research as on ethnographic fieldwork. Its theoretical approach is that of political economy and world systems theory, both of which look at the connection between wealth and power.

Who is right? If both sides of a debate are carefully considered and their arguments clearly set out, then the answer usually is both. In this particular debate, given the wide diversity in the ecological, economic, social and political patterns of Bushmen groups over southern Africa as well as the variety of historical and contact experiences they have had over time, either of the approaches may be the more appropriate.

Some groups, such as the Ju/'hoansi of the Dobe–Nyae Nyae region of north-western Botswana and north-eastern Namibia, have been quite isolated and retained the foraging way of life. Others, such as the Bushmen of the Ghanzi district in Botswana, have had some contact, especially through trade, without its having had much effect on their way of life. Yet others, especially in the northern and eastern Kalahari, have had intensive and prolonged contact, with transforming effects on their society and culture. The field of Bushman and hunter-gatherer studies would benefit if these two approaches were combined, rather than remaining in opposition.

cantly towards gender equality in Bushman society. Women generally share with their families the supply of plant foods, which, depending on the time of year, they may gather daily or twice a week.

The men, who provide the more sought-after food item, share out the meat they bring in amongst a wider circle of people. If there is a large carcass the circle of distribution may include members from other bands. The division of meat becomes an important means of sharing and discharging one's social debts, as well as of enacting the important values of being generous, returning gifts and not boasting. People display their social skills on such an occasion, but it may also trigger tension and fights, followed perhaps by trance dancing to cool down tempers and restore harmony.

As well as forming the favourite food item, animals feed the mind. Bushmen are quite fascinated by them; they are the principal characters in myth and lore and may embody spiritual power and spirit beings. The hunt becomes a metaphor for marriage; in some of the folktales about the antelope, the hunter's quarry becomes his 'animal wife'. The hunt is also a key symbol or act in healing and initiation ritual. Animals were painted or engraved extensively on rock surfaces and continue to be the chosen motifs for contemporary Bushman artists.

Ecological adaptations

Keeping the birth rate down is another way of adjusting to the environment's limited resources in the Kalahari. Prolonged nursing of children, combined with the lactating mother's low stores of body fat, reduces ovulation and prevents conception. This results in wide birth spacing, of up to three or four years.

Whenever local resources are exhausted the mobile and flexible lifestyle of the people and the variable composition of the group allow them to move on. They follow migratory game and move from places where the rains fail and where there is little plant food to better favoured areas. Such moves may take a band outside its own n!ore.

Social factors as much as ecological ones are part of the Bushmen's adaptive strategies. Ownership of land and resources, territorial boundaries and group membership, all need to be open and flexible to allow neighbouring bands access to one another's land. This is what we find among Kalahari Bushmen. N!ore boundaries overlap, and reciprocal access to resources is granted (to those asking politely). Moreover, land ownership is loosely defined; the 'owner' or 'master' (kxao) of a

territory, or of a permanent water hole that defines it, exercises a form of 'responsible stewardship', making the Ju/'hoan kxao, in the words of Richard Katz, Megan Biesele and Verna St Denis, 'more an informed person who can care for a water resource so that it can be shared than an exclusive holder of rights to that water'.

These adaptive, risk-managing mechanisms are especially active in the dry season, when more than one band might move to the site of a permanent water hole and spend weeks or months in each other's company. This time is spent in renewing social ties with neighbouring band members. It provides the ideal occasion for brokering marriages between members of bands that are exogamous – that is, who are required to marry outside their own group. The time is also ideal for holding such ritual activities as trance dancing and male initiation ceremonies, which are more effective or efficient when conducted with a large number of participants. Another activity that is intensified whenever people get together in multi-band groupings is a form of exchange called xaro by the Ju/'hoansi.

Social organisation

In xaro we see the operation of the key values of Bushman society. They share, co-operate, reciprocate and, by favouring the circulation of goods amongst many rather than the accumulation by one or a few, they also exhibit egalitarianism. As a system of networks centred upon the individual, the formal organisation of xaro points to yet another set of values: individualism and personal autonomy. These values match the 'familistic' social organisation of the Ju/'hoansi and other Kalahari Bushmen.

The bands, which are the core of their societies, are made up of a group of siblings, with their spouses and, for a time, their parents, more or less aged. Such a group maintains, in the loose and non-exclusive manner described above, ownership and control over a water hole and n!ore. In tune with the seasons the group exploits its resources in small family groups or camps or in larger groupings that may be joined by others. There is a strong bond of kinship amongst the members of a band, and through marriage with members of other bands. It is regulated by two types of kin relations: a 'joking' relationship and an 'avoidance' relationship.

The joking relationship is between certain members of a person's own generation: same-sex siblings, spouses, opposite-sex siblings-in-law, as well as members of one's alternate generation: grandparents and grandchildren. Another expression of emotional closeness to such relatives is that ideally an individual gets his or her name from a grandparent.

Respect and formality set the tone of the 'avoidance' relationship, towards kin in the ascending generations: one's parents and their siblings, and one's children and, upon marriage, their in-law counterparts.

The Ju/'hoansi have a unique mechanism, the name or namesake relationship, for extending kin terms to a wide range of non-relatives. All individuals sharing one of the thirty-odd sex-linked names are considered to be kin. Since three-quarters of Ju/'hoan men and women bear one or another of the dozen or so most popular names, the range of name-relatives becomes very wide indeed. Namesake kin stand in a joking relationship to each other; those older are treated as though they were grandparents, those younger as grandchildren.

Marriages are arranged by the parents of the prospective couple, usually when both are still small children. Such betrothals are sealed with an

---

26 • Insulting the meat •

The following is Richard Lee's account (in his book The Dobe Ju/'hoansi) of this levelling mechanism, as explained to him by the Ju/'hoansi.

Men are encouraged to hunt as well as they can, and the people are happy when the meat is brought in, but the correct demeanor for the successful hunter is modesty and understatement. A /Xai/xai man named /Gaugo said:

'Say that a man has been hunting. He must not come home and announce like a braggart, "I have killed a big one in the bush!" He must first sit down in silence until I or someone else comes up to his fire and asks, "What did you see today?"

'He replies quietly, "Ah, I'm no good for hunting. I saw nothing at all … maybe just a tiny one."

'Then I smile to myself because I know he has killed something big.'

The theme of modesty is continued when the butchering and carrying party goes to fetch the kill the following day. Arriving at the site, the members of the carrying party loudly express their disappointment to the hunter.

'You, man, you have dragged us all the way out here to make us cart home your pile of bones? Oh, if I had known it was this thin I

wouldn't have come. People, to think that I gave up a nice day in the shade for this. At home we may be hungry, but at least we have nice cool water to drink.'

To these insults the hunter must not act offended; he should respond with self-demeaning words:

'You're right, this one is not worth the effort; let's just cook the liver for strength and leave the rest for the hyenas. It's not too late to hunt today, and even a duiker or steenbok would be better than this mess.'

The party, of course, has no intention of abandoning the kill. The heavy joking and derision are directed toward one goal: the levelling of potentially arrogant behaviour in a successful hunter. The !Kung recognise the tendency toward arrogance and take definite steps to combat it. As ≠Tomzho, the famous healer from /Xai/xai, put it:

'When a young man kills much meat, he comes to think of himself as a chief or big man, and he thinks the rest of us are his servants or inferiors. We can't accept this. We refuse one who boasts, for some day his pride will make him kill somebody. So we always speak of his meat as worthless. In this way we cool his heart and make him gentle.'

8.4: *The early stage of a healing dance at Dobe in 1964.*

8.5: *The healing dance continues.*

exchange of gifts. These plans have to take into account the prohibitions on partners who are within the kinship and namesake systems. These are extensive and reduce the number of suitable partners. Upon marriage the young couple usually live with the parents of the bride. The bride might still be a young, pre-pubescent girl. The husband hunts for his in-laws, showing that he is able to provide for his wife and children-to-be. After the birth of the first or second child the couple have the option of moving to another band, perhaps the husband's or that of other kin or friends.

These arranged marriages frequently fail, having been made against the wishes of the principals, especially the girl who, being so much younger than the man, is less able to assert herself. The wife usually initiates the dissolution of a marriage – another example of the independence of women in Bushman society. Dissolving one's marriage, and entering a new marriage, are both straightforward, unceremonious procedures.

Leadership, decision-making and conflict resolution

Because of the egalitarian nature of Bushman society, leadership is loosely institutionalised. Some societies appear to have had no leaders of any sort, like the G/wi, amongst whom, according to George Silberbauer, 'every member of the band has rights equal to those of all others'. But a Bushman band usually has a tenuous authority figure, the headman. He is 'as thin as the rest', as Lorna Marshall observed among the Ju/'hoansi, and has no special privileges or insignia of office. That office is achieved, not ascribed or inherited; the headman holds what little authority he has through personal popularity, wisdom and his ability to speak well, all of which enable him to give sound advice and good counsel. When decisions are made, or a dispute is dealt with, he may not dominate the discussion, let alone exercise any pressure on the group. The deliberations are a free-for-all, to which everyone adds his voice – and hers, women being very much part of the decision-making process. The aim is to reach a decision that all can live with, since all have had a say in it.

Was this always so in the past? We can probably assume that, as a general principle, leadership roles have not changed. There are historically doc-umented circumstances, however, where leadership was invested. The nineteenth-century leader ≠Dukuri may have gained his position as war chief by uniting the ≠Au//eisi and //Aikwe into a formidable fighting force against the raids and attempted incursion on their lands by agropastoralists in the 1800s.

While historical details of Bushman resistance to trekboer encroachment in the interior of South Africa in the 1700s reflect only the colonial viewpoint, the historian Nigel Penn says that the General Commando was organised by white farmers against 'a most threatening and no doubt concerted campaign of resistance'. The commando failed in all but its immediate objectives to control the Bushmen. The Bushmen were able to keep up their fierce war with a great deal of success. We are uncertain whether they were able to cohere under war leaders, but there is a possibility that this was indeed the case.

A leader who arose to fill a need was not necessarily able to sustain this function after the need disappeared. And certainly the war leadership of ≠Dukuri did not create a permanent political hierarchy. By the late 1800s the centralised authority of the war leadership had disappeared and the Nharo reverted to an egalitarian society.

Nowadays an 'uppity' leader is brought into line, through ridicule, criticism and non-compliance. Ambitiousness, arrogance, boastfulness, all go against the 'humility ethos' of the Ju/'hoansi – one of the ideological controls, or 'levelling mechanisms', through which social equality is maintained.

Much the same treatment is given to a good and successful hunter, especially a young and overeager one, who may be inclined to boast about his accomplishment in bringing down a big animal, and about the quantity and fatness of the meat. Instead, he is expected, according to Ju/'hoan values, to 'insult the meat', lest it is he who becomes the target of insults!

As ≠Tomzho suggested (see Box 26), such levelling mechanisms also contribute towards reducing conflict. Given the strong individualism of people, conflict is as ready to erupt as it is dreaded. Conflict within this familistic society, in which bonds of co-operation are vital for the group's survival, is disruptive and avoided as much as possible because it holds the potential for violence in a

8.6: *A woman trancer.*

hunting culture where spears, knives and poison arrows are readily at hand.

When conflict does erupt over stinginess, improper sharing or *xaro* or kinship behaviour, shirking of work or arrogance, attempts are first made to deal with the issue discreetly and circumspectly. This allows the individual targeted for censure to save face.

'Talking' is one approach taken in or out of earshot of the person at fault. A number of ploys may be used: influencing opinion, the 'forced eavesdrop', or 'auditory withdrawal'. Members of the group handle conflict by invoking informal sanctions and subtle pressure to restore harmony. Joking, teasing and laughter may be another way of expressing censure, in which the censured party's joking partner often plays a part.

However, as Richard Lee has noticed among the Ju/'hoansi, this 'talking' approach to conflict, which the Ju/'hoansi call *horehore* or *obaoba* (translated as 'yakity-yak'), may, for all its apparent jocularity, be quite serious, 'proceed[ing] along the knife edge between laughter and danger'.

The 'withdrawal option' is a solution readily available to these nomadic people, who live in societies with variable group composition. One party in a dispute that cannot be settled packs its things and leaves the group either permanently, or to return weeks or months later with the conflict, ideally, forgotten and forgiven.

Ritual

Another effective way for dealing with social tensions in the group is through the trance healing dance. Megan Biesele has shown how a Ju/'hoan trance dancer, in the process of curing a person, may also pointedly address himself to issues of conflict pending in the group. Women, who make up the clapping and singing circle around which the healers dance themselves into trance, may also bring up issues of 'stinginess' or 'bad manners' during the dance. Their angry exchanges may dominate the dance for a while, temporarily bringing their chanting to a halt, and be resumed only after 'talking' has calmed tempers. They may also contrive to place side by side two women at odds with each other.

Curing, the real reason for the dance, is carried out when dancers are near or in trance. This is said to activate the healing potency in the dancer's stomach. It is called *n/om* (or *n/um*) by the Ju/'hoansi; other Bushman groups use different terms for this widely known notion, such as *tsso*, the Nharo term. Trance (*!kia*, or *!aia*) brings *n/om* to a boil and as the trance state intensifies, it works its way up the dancer's spinal cord, to 'explode' in his brain. It is exuded from his body through sweat, which is then rubbed over the patient's body. Another way of treating disease is to suck it out of the body. Dancers consider the experience of *!aia* extremely painful, as well as dangerous; they liken it to the experience of dying.

While most of the dancers are men, of whom about half have experienced trance, trance dancing is not exclusive to men. About a third of Ju/'hoan women have experienced trance, although the Nharo consider women's healing potency less 'strong' than men's and regard women's ritual strength to lie more in singing. Singing is the essential trigger for trancing. Nharo dancers will often call to the women with plaintive voices to step up their singing lest trance elude them. A generation ago the Ju/'hoan women acquired their own curing dance, the drum dance. This reverses the normal gender roles. The women dance and trance, and the men provide the music. This is another instance of gender equality within Bushman social organisation and culture, and of women asserting their independence.

The night-long dances, the clapping and singing of the women, the dancers' piercing shrieks at the moment of trance collapse, the stamping of the dancers' feet, their rhythm accentuated by the rattles they wear around their feet, and the attendance of many engrossed people, all make for a dramatic performance. A trance dance is an instance of 'community healing' and, more generally, a 'rite of solidarity' that expresses and reinforces the values of sharing, co-operation and egalitarianism. It is an expression of the symbols and beliefs of Bushman spiritual culture as the trance dancer, like shamans everywhere in the world, enters the spirit realm while he is in trance. When he lies collapsed on the ground, dancers 'slip out of their skins' and their spirits, at grave peril, will seek out the spirits of the dead and other spirit beings to get them to return health and well-being to people. A dancer may transform himself into an animal, an antelope or a lion, in order to be able to carry out

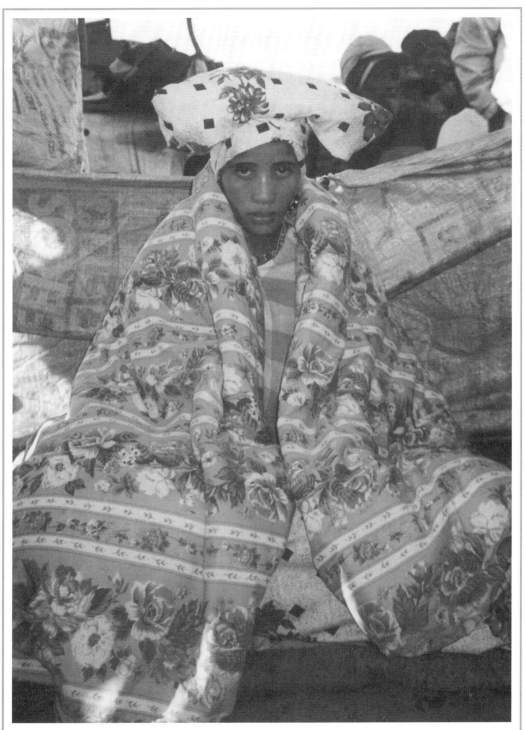

8.7: *Young Bushman girl in Herero dress undergoing a female initiation rite. Among the Herero, with whom the Bushmen of the Omaheke district have close ties, one of the signs of womanhood is the kind of dress pictured above and the wide-brimmed hat.*

his 'extra-body travel' more rapidly.

Antelopes are a mystical presence at both male and female Bushman initiation rites. The male rite is a hunting ritual that revolves around the young man hunting his 'First Buck', an event filled with symbols and ritual. To improve his hunting skills the young man has tattoo-like cuts administered to various parts of his body, into which is rubbed 'medicine' made of fat and charred herbs.

Among a number of Bushman groups one of the ritual highlights of the girl's initiation, performed at her first menstruation, is the 'eland dance'. An old man wearing antelope horns (or branches in imitation) uses dancing steps to look like an eland bull and 'chases' the women around the girl's menstrual hut. The women mimic the female eland by lifting their skirts and baring their buttocks.

Unlike the male rite, which for most Bushman groups was probably optional, the female initiation rite was an indispensable part of the young woman's life cycle. The relative importance of the two sets of initiation rites is shown by the fact that

27 • The Bushman trickster •

This figure is universal in the myths and tales of the Bushmen and the Khoekhoen. The traits and actions of the trickster are multiple, ranging from those of lewd prankster to divine creator, from goblin to god, human to jackal, incarnation within the lowest of animals, the louse, to Spirit Keeper of the highest, the eland.

He has almost as many names as he has guises, such as /Kaggen, Pate, Pisamboro, Kaoxa (or ≠Gao!na) and //Guwa (or several versions of the word). The Khoekhoen called him Haiseb (Heitsi-aibib) or Jackal. The last is a favourite also in the tales of the Ghanzi farm Bushmen, who refer to this figure by its Afrikaans name, Jakkals.

As a classic prankster – a role he occupies in the oral traditions of people all over the world – he plays practical, at times malicious and often obscene jokes on others, delighting in their misfortune. He violates social norms and taboos, through acts of incest, lewdness, gluttony, selfishness and boastfulness. In this way he creates a social and moral state of topsy-turvydom.

There are other sides to the Bushman trickster. While he may hurt and even kill beings around him, he may also turn towards them as 'Spirit Protector'. He is a culture hero who has brought water holes and river beds to the Kalahari, as well as fire, cooking and 'carnal knowledge' to humans; and he gave some ani-

mals their distinctive traits. In fact, in some tales he is the creative agent who has brought about the present order of existence, in which humans are humans and animals animals. It should be noted, however, that today's creatures, humans and animals, retain, in the stories and beliefs, memories of one another's former state of being. This may explain in part why Bushmen feel so drawn to animals.

The trickster also shuttles back and forth between the mythological past and the historical present, which he visits as the farm hand, Jakkals, tricking his Afrikaner *baas*. In every way the trickster is the 'embodiment of ambiguity' and a 'lord of disorder'.

A number of Khoesaan people believe that the trickster is also a divinity. Early missionaries, to their considerable consternation, were told by their Khoekhoe converts that Heitsi-aibib is 'our Jesus of olden times'. They likened the figure to the devil, a misconception that missionaries and christianised Bushmen may hold to this day. //Guwa controls diseases and their cure (through the offices of the trance dancer) and he may be present at initiation rites. Some Bushman groups believe that he protects animals from danger or abuse by hunters. He can inspire awe and reverence in people, in contrast to the frivolity and outrage he can elicit as the teller of stories.

the male rite is now only a memory amongst the farm Bushmen while the female rite continues to be practised along with a shortened version of the eland dance. As recently as June 1997 I witnessed a performance in the ≠Au//eisi section of Epako, the Gobabis township.

Myth and belief

Being consummate storytellers, Bushmen have a rich store of myth and lore, with much interpersonal, intergroup and interregional variation. A few common threads can be isolated.

One is the idea of an earlier order of creation or existence in which spirit beings, humans and animals were not separate but intermingled. They were either hybrid beings – human–animals of every description and from every animal phylum – or shape-shifting beings. These beings are like the 'therioanthropic' figures seen in rock art and by the trance dancer when he experiences a spiritual transformation. Rock art abounds in literal, mystical or metaphorical depictions of the trance dance. It shows the close intermingling, in Bushman symbolic and expressive culture, of myth, art and ritual. In Bushman myth and belief the ambiguity in the make-up of mythological times and ritual states is embodied in the trickster.

CHAPTER NINE

Hunter-gatherers in transition

Because so many of the Bushman groups on the Kalahari fringes have not followed the 'classic' foraging way of life for over a century, it is difficult to pinpoint when or where the transition from hunting-gathering to sedentary food production occurred. Most Bushmen in southern Africa have never been static in their social, economic and cultural forms. They have probably always experienced 'transition' of some sort. The transition described here is that from pre-colonial to post-colonial foraging or, at the Kalahari fringes, foraging alongside agropastoralism. It has led to modern post-foraging ways of living, such as village, reserve or settlement life, farming and herding, wage labour and other forms of employment.

These changes took place at the same time as a growing sense of political awareness and action on the part of the Bushmen, who now live as ethnic minorities in independent and democratic nation states. These states have found themselves less and less able to ignore the political and land rights of their Bushman citizens.

9.1: *N!aba, a Ghanzi farm Bushwoman, photographed in June 1995.*

Farm labour

Before the changes of the last eight or ten years, the political position of the Bushmen in Botswana and Namibia, as well as Angola, Zambia, Zimbabwe and, most recently, South Africa, was considerably more passive, in spite of economic depression and political oppression. The actions and policies of these post-colonial governments were those of benign, and in some cases not so benign, neglect.

In Botswana and Namibia, the countries with the largest Bushman populations, socio-economic change for the Bushmen during most of the twentieth century occurred primarily in the context of farm labour on German, Afrikaner or English cattle ranches. Most of these were in the Grootfontein, Gobabis and Ghanzi districts of Namibia (until 1990, South West Africa) and Botswana (until 1966, Bechuanaland). Bushmen in the Mier region of the Northern Cape were also drawn into farm labour when Baster sheep farmers were allocated the land in 1930 and hired the dispossessed local ≠Khomeni Bushmen as labourers.

Farmers in all these regions were dependent on Bushman labour. The anthropologist Robert Gordon reports that in 1975 as many as 88 per cent of all Bushmen in Namibia were in the employ of white farmers. The treatment of farm Bushmen by farmers was sometimes brutal, especially when labourers had been forced into service because they had been found without the pass each Bushman was required to carry. This regulation was introduced by the South African administration of South West Africa a few years after they took the territory over from the Germans (in 1915), to control vagrancy and squatting.

Another way of forcing Bushmen into farm labour was out-and-out kidnapping ('black-birding'), a practice that appears to have continued in the Gobabis (now Omaheke) district until the mid-1950s.

For the first fifty years of contact in the Ghanzi district the relationship between white farmer and Bushman labourer was somewhat more benign, despite exploitative working conditions. Wages consisted of small cash sums or food rations or both, as well as, on some farms, a calf or two. Farmers hoped that having his own animals in

9.2: *!Khuma//ka, husband of N!aba.*

28 • My Bushman 'parents' •

My wife, Patricia, and I lived in a cow-dung hut at D'Kar village from 1968 to 1970. !Khuma//ka and N!aba were our next-door neighbours. I was doing ethnographic field-work for my doctorate and my wife, a registered nurse, was operating the clinic attached to the mission station of which D'Kar village was a part.

The Nharo couple were in their late fifties at the time and had been married for over twenty years. They had had nine children (four sons and five daughters), of whom two daughters had died as infants. Most of the children were grown up at the time we were there. The younger ones and some small grandchildren lived with them. One or other of them was always sick, seeking help from my wife. She also treated N!aba on a few occasions for various aches and pains, and assisted in the birth of two of her grandchildren.

Another regular patient of Patricia's was !Khuma//ka himself, who had bad arthritis in his legs. This disability had cut short his career as a farm labourer on Ghanzi farms. With time on his hands !Khuma//ka had elected to spend much of it with me, initially as one of my Nharo language teachers. He was interested in his people's folktales. Trickster stories especially appealed to his earthy sense of humour and he enjoyed stories about events from his childhood (at the 'time of the wagons', i.e. before the arrival of trucks).

A number of his tales were about his father, who had taught him archery, hunting and bush lore, or about himself as a young man, working for Afrikaner or English farmers. His stories about his employers were often elaborate. He referred to them by nicknames: 'Spring Hare', 'Ostrich Hen', 'Ostrich Penis',

'Pail', 'Tortoise Neck', 'Eggshell Head'. He impersonated some of them with uncanny fidelity, adding snippets of Afrikaans, which he speaks quite well, and English, which he doesn't but can imitate phonetically – and hilariously. A bit like me speaking Nharo, he suggested wryly and, I must confess, not altogether inaccurately. !Khuma//ka is still a consummate storyteller and at my last visit, in 1997, I collected some more tales, or versions of previous stories, from him.

Patricia's experiences with N!aba and mine with !Khuma//ka, who early on became my 'key informant' whose company, knowledge, experience and humour I soon came to appreciate, resulted in the establishment of a mutual friendship. About half a year into our stay at D'Kar they announced to us that we would henceforth be 'their children'. They gave us Bushman names: Di/'kgao for my wife, Kãkn//ai for me. It is interesting to note that both names were drawn not from their own children's generation, but from that of their grandchildren (as well as their grandparents). We were, by this practice, brought into a joking relationship to our new parents who, in terms of the logic of their kinship and naming patterns, were actually our grandparents.

We've kept in touch with them over the years. Sadly !Nabe recently died of cancer. When I saw her last in 1997 she had just assisted her grandson and his wife to choose names for their first child.

!Khuma//ka, now well into his eighties, is the respected elder of a large family that is now three generations deep. A recent communication from a mutual friend in D'Kar informs me that he is looking for a new wife!

their herds might increase the Bushman herder's diligence.

The relationship between labourer and employer was paternalistic, modelled on that of the first

generation of Boer settlers who arrived at Ghanzi just before the turn of the century. A white rancher hired 'his' Bushman labourers and 'looked after' their families, who all lived in the small village of grass or cow-dung huts adjacent to the farmhouse. Some of the Bushwomen performed domestic service for the farmer's wife. Younger women might be entrusted with looking after the farmer's children, a practice that continued in Ghanzi until a generation ago. A Bushman family might stay in the same family's service for several generations. This form of 'patron–client' or 'hereditary service' relationship between Boer and Bushman, in the context of an ideology of social and moral superiority, resembles the labour pattern between Bushmen and other herding people into whose economic and political orbit the former were drawn.

Bushmen and cattle people

All herding people of southern Africa, whether Khoekhoen or Bantu-speaking, have looked down on the stockless Bushmen. This is partly because of the 'Bushman problem', as ranchers and administrators in Namibia and Botswana have liked to refer to it: both cattle and antelopes use the same grazing, and cattle crush veld food plants with their hoofs. Moreover, wild and domestic grazers, as well as people, use the same water points. This competition for resources results in conflict and resistance.

Another reason is ideological: herding people consider foraging to be an inferior mode of existence, practised by vagrant riff-raff and good-for-nothings. The idea that hunting-gathering is an unproductive, non-legitimate use of land is voiced by some government officials even today, with harmful consequences for the cause of Bushman land rights. This attitude is also reflected in the Tswana people's term for the Bushmen, 'Basarwa', which Alice Mogwe, the Botswanan human rights advocate, describes as 'those who have not acquired any cattle'. The earlier term 'Masarwa' also indicates social inferiority. Its prefix 'ma' denotes subservience, and its presumed root 'tua' means 'despised neighbouring tribe'.

Although the Tswana considered them inferior and undesirable, they incorporated neighbouring Bushmen into their economy and society. Bushmen occupied the lowest rung of the Tswana social hierarchy, a form of serfdom the Tswana call *bothlanka*. Apart from paying tribute in the form of ivory, venison and ostrich feathers, the pre-

colonial *bothla* serfs also had to render labour service, especially as cattle herders and farm workers. Bushman cattle herders were given milk but no remuneration. Indeed, they were brutally punished whenever an animal went astray or was killed by lions. Bushman families were 'owned' by their Tswana masters and bequeathed as property to their sons. Although no master had the right to sell or buy a serf, Bushchildren were sometimes sold as slaves to colonists in the Cape Colony to the south. Eventually these oppressive practices were relaxed after pressure from the British colonial government and, later, from the League of Nations to whose attention reports of alleged slavery had been brought.

The payment of cattle for labour was introduced by the Tswana chiefdom of the Ngwato under Khama III, who later also abolished the payment of tribute by the 'Masarwa'. Similar policies were adopted by two other Tswana chiefdoms, the Ngwaketse and the Kwena. According to the Tswana *mafisa* system, when a stock-owner leaves his cattle to be looked after by another person, the latter can drink the milk, take some of the calves born in the course of the arrangement, eat the meat of beasts that die naturally, and use the animals for ploughing.

In the late 1950s and through the 1960s the paternalistic labour pattern on the Ghanzi farms changed, though not for the better. After more farms were surveyed and offered as freehold leases to outside ranchers, a new type of farmer came to the district. Many of these were of English (South African) descent and they brought with them capital, new breeds of stock and modernised, mechanised methods of ranching. This meant that a smaller and more skilled labour force was required on the farms. The new ranchers hired black and coloured workers, whom they deemed more skilled and reliable for cattle and wage labour.

As a result many Bushmen became or remained unemployed and were left without any place to stay. Living on a farm without working for the owner was, and still is, considered squatting. Poverty, hunger, malnutrition, disease (especially affecting small children), as well as fighting, prostitution, arrest (often for suspected stock theft) and alcohol abuse became increasing problems for the Ghanzi farm Bushmen of the 1960s. While less prevalent today, thanks to initiatives by both government and non-government organisations, they remain problems for many farm Bushmen, both in the Ghanzi district and in the Omaheke district across the border in Namibia.

The trance dance and cultural revitalisation

Trance dancing among Ghanzi farm Bushmen rose markedly in incidence and intensity in the late 1960s. This was a response to the greater number of people falling ill as a result of malnutrition, tuberculosis and venereal diseases, and because of witchcraft and sorcery (a form of psychosomatic illness the Bushmen did not suffer from previously). Another reason is that a ritual of such great emotional and spiritual force appealed to an impoverished, bitter and hopeless people. Farm Bushmen see trance dancing as very much 'Bushmanwork'. It is a cultural event that defines, dramatically and poignantly, the identity of the Bushman people within the pluralist society of Ghanzi and the country as a whole. The Tswana and Herero sometimes attend trance dances and submit to the ministrations of a trance dancer, as 'Bushman medicine' is held to be strong.

Because there is so much trance dancing, the numbers of dancers, songs and dance styles, and the range of mystical diseases identified and treated, have increased. Some dancers exclude witchcraft and sorcery from their field of expertise, while others include it. The giraffe dance, which the Ghanzi Bushmen probably obtained from the Ju/'hoansi, is still performed and generally seen as the 'classic' Bushman dance. However, it now has to compete with a number of other dances, and with alternative approaches to healing (such as herbal remedies and potions).

Most Bushman healers now charge fees, which may be very high. Those with the best reputation may demand a goat or two, or one or two weeks' wages. This commercialism is in marked contrast to the spirit of communalism, sharing and service in which the dance was previously performed.

Some of the less renowned dancers offer scaled-down curing dance performances. The performance may be reduced from the usual ten to twelve hours from dusk to dawn, to just two or three hours. Some perform shortened dances, per-

9.3: *A trance curing dance photographed at Gobabis.*

9.4: *A camp scene at the village of /Xai/xai, 1968.*

haps during the day instead of at night, without a fire or a circle of participants other than those around the hut of the sick person on whose behalf the dance is held.

Their more distinguished colleagues still continue the grand style of trance dancing. The Ghanzi farm Bushmen admire the dancers of renown for their curing abilities, their spiritual knowledge and insights, and their courage and stamina in braving 'death' by embarking on spiritual journeys to the beyond. But they also admire them for their independence and wealth, earned not by working for the *buuru* (Boer), but by doing a 'Bushman thing'.

A similar process, in which the trance dance and dancer become vehicles for dealing with and expressing the economic and political frustrations and aspirations of the people, was observed among the Ju/'hoansi of the crowded village of /Kae/kae (/Xai/xai). In 1997 the psychologist Richard Katz returned there with Megan Biesele and Verna St Denis for a follow-up on the trance dance study he had carried out there a generation earlier. Like the Ghanzi farm Bushmen, the /Kae/kae people lived in a state of poverty, hunger, sickness and oppres-

sion from Herero and Tswana pastoralists, who had become the holders of wealth and power in the region. The 'synergetic', cathartic, energising, morally integrating and value-asserting qualities of the dance Katz had observed earlier were noticed again. The key difference is that the trance dancers, whose role is now more professionalised than it had been before, have become the community's spokespersons on issues of political rights and land.

Government policies

In both Botswana and Namibia the policies that have had the most direct impact on the Bushmen were those relating to land. In Botswana, land reforms introduced by the post-colonial government rendered land allocations more democratic and boosted the cattle industry, the economic mainstay of the country. In Namibia the land policies of the South African administration involved setting up ethnically based territories, in line with the apartheid master plan of 'separate development'.

9.5: *Schmidtsdrift, June 1995.*

The early South African administration of Namibia introduced regulations to control Bushman cattle theft, squatting, labour and hunting rights. These were quite harsh and punitive and affected individuals directly. But the effects of the new land policies were even more damaging as they affected Bushmen as a group. They led to massive land losses, and set the conditions for a state of economic impoverishment and political impotence that has lasted to this day.

A number of commissions were established: the Native Reserve Commission in 1921; the Commission for the Protection of the Bushmen in 1949; and the Odendaal Commission in 1963, which decided whether reserves should be set aside for the different ethnic groups of the country. Whereas one Bushman group, the Hai//om around Etosha, received no land at all, a territory called 'Bushmanland' was set up for the Ju/'hoansi in 1970 (today known as Eastern Otjozondjupa). At under 6000 square kilometres, the territory would sustain only 170 Bushmen, were they to follow traditional foraging, which requires band territo-

ries ranging in size from 500 to 1000 square kilometres. Yet two thousand people live there. Outside herders continued to enter the area, as they had done before it was 'reserved' for the Ju/'hoansi. The territories that had been assigned to the Herero in the south and the Kavango in the north all made deep inroads on lands previously occupied by the Ju/'hoansi. Moreover, a portion of the land was designated as a game park, the Kaudom Game Reserve.

Apart from these land divisions and allocations, in the late 1950s the South African administration also created a Bushman reserve at Tsumkwe, a water hole around which a band of two to three dozen Ju/'hoan foragers had lived before. By the 1970s about a thousand people lived there, half the entire population of Bushmanland. By the 1980s the place had become overcrowded and beset with apathy and poverty, conflict, jealousies, fighting and alcohol abuse. People began to leave a community that had become a rural slum. It is interesting to note that the film 'The Gods Must be Crazy', which depicts the Bushmen in ultra-

29 • Bushman soldiers in South African uniform •

Two SADF bases were established, one at Omega in the Caprivi in 1975, the other at Tsumkwe (now written as Tjum!kui) in Bushmanland in 1978. The Tsumkwe base was later moved to Mangetti Dune, because of water shortage and tensions between the local Ju/'hoansi and the Angolan !O!Kung. Ten thousand soldiers and their dependants lived at the sixteen settlements around these bases. The Bushman people in both regions developed strong dependence on the army, which placed itself in the role of a development agency, providing boreholes, agricultural plots, and medical, educational and religious services, as well as building houses and schools. When Namibia became independent in 1990, the Bushman soldiers and their families were given the choice by the SADF of returning with them to South Africa, where the army would continue to 'look after' them. Four thousand went, into what was for them a foreign land and an uncertain future.

They were settled at the army tent city of Schmidtsdrift west of Kimberley. This was a temporary measure, as the site was in the process of being reclaimed by the Tswana community of the Tlhaping, who had been removed from the region in 1968. Despite the efforts at community development by the South African advocacy group, the !Xu and Khwe Trust, which had become established at Schmidtsdrift, community life at this temporary tent settlement was beset with social conflict, including sorcery and elder abuse. A further problem was a lack of resources such as hunting rights and wild plant foods and firewood on the land around Schmidtsdrift.

romantic terms as 'flower children of the Kalahari' doing battle with a bottle from the sky, was filmed at Tsumkwe at that period in the community's life. A more realistic film, and one a good deal more moving and poignant, is John Marshall's 'N!ai, the Story of a !Kung Woman'.

Another government action that was to have a strong impact on the Bushmen in the last decade of South African rule was the drafting of Bushman soldiers into the South African Defence Force (SADF). Some of them were !O!Kung and Kxoe Bushmen from Angola who had fled across the Namibian border after reprisal actions against them by the new Angolan government, which, after a fourteen-year freedom struggle against the Portuguese, took over power in 1975.

The first land reform in Botswana, introduced two years after independence, was the Tribal Land Act of 1968. This Act transferred the authority to allocate land within tribal territories from traditional leaders to the democratic institution of the local district Land Boards. Recipients of land were the tribal members of each region. But the Bushmen were excluded. As ethnic outsiders they were not considered to be 'tribesmen'.

The land rights of the Bushmen continued to be a key concern of the Remote Areas Development Programme set up by the government in 1974. First called the Bushman Development Programme, its purpose was to seek to understand and deal with the problems and needs of Botswana's rural poor. In an attempt to avoid official ethnic labels for its citizens in the multiracial, democratic country of Botswana, these rural poor, the majority of them Bushmen, were called 'Remote Area Dwellers' (RADs). However, despite the efforts of the RAD Officer regarding Bushman land rights, all that could be secured were small pieces of land (ranging from 16 to 500 square kilometres), on which government-sponsored settlements were set up for the Bushmen, along with such social services as schools, clinics and food aid programmes.

As at Tsumkwe in Namibia, these settlements were soon overcrowded and the land provided was inadequate for foraging. The overcrowding problem has been exacerbated by outsiders. Non-Bushman cattle herders moved to the RAD settlements at such a rate that some of them have become their cattle posts where, in the words of

30 • Land to people (with cattle): The TGLP •

This account of the TGLP by Bob Hitchcock and John Holm comes from one of their reports on the state of the Bushmen to the American indigenous rights organisation 'Cultural Survival', in the publication Cultural Survival Quarterly.

In 1975, the government of Botswana announced a land reform and livestock programme known as the Tribal Grazing Land Policy (TGLP). Its purpose was to (1) prevent further range degradation, (2) reduce income disparities between rich and poor, and (3) facilitate the commercialisation and growth of the livestock industry. In order to achieve these goals, a process of commercialisation or privatisation of the tribal land was to be carried out. Leasehold rights over blocks of land were to be granted on a long-term basis in exchange for nominal rent payments.

The Bushmen did not benefit from the land tenure change, however. While the 1975 government White Paper stated that the rural poor's land needs would be met, the only provision made for them was the establishment of the so-called 'Reserved Areas'. When the zoning process was completed, it was found that no land whatsoever had been set aside as reserved. Anthropologists and a few government administrators had asked that some land be set aside within commercial areas so that people could have access to land for social services and for generating income and subsistence. But as in the case of the government settlement schemes, the land set aside was woefully inadequate. Dispossession has already occurred in several parts of Botswana where ranches were established under the TGLP. If this continues, it is possible that as much as a fourth of the entire Bushman population of Botswana will lose their land.

Bob Hitchcock, 'large stock owners get free water paid for out of donor funds or Domestic Development Funds'.

The Bushman headmen whom the government have set up as official authority figures at each of the settlements have credibility and legitimacy problems among both their own people and non-Bushman village members when they attempt to carry out official duties. In egalitarian societies there are cultural barriers against an 'officious' style of leadership. In addition, lack of education and literacy have hampered these gazetted leaders in their dealings with government.

The deplorable conditions faced by some of Botswana's Bushman people are made worse by another government land reform initiative, the Tribal Grazing Land Policy (TGLP).

Insecure land tenure or, even worse, forced expropriation and relocation either by government or cattle owners 'invading' what little land the Bushman are allowed to lay claim to, continue to be the burning concerns of the Bushmen of Botswana and Namibia. They are at the head of the political demands of the Bushman communities of these two countries and of South Africa.

CHAPTER TEN

The present and future of post-foraging Bushmen

Even though many problems remain, in the 1990s some advances have been made both in terms of development and politically in the lives of today's largely post-foraging Bushmen. Their status, stance and state have changed from that of social marginals who are discriminated against to citizens holding a strong sense of cultural identity and ethnic pride; from political passivity and submissiveness to action and assertiveness; from economic dependence to self-sufficiency.

Developments of promise

Regarding their legal status, Botswana's discriminatory Tribal Land Act, which favoured non-Bushmen in the allocation of land – and by extension, through the TGLP, also the acquiring of cattle – was amended on 30 October 1993. The word 'tribesmen', defining those eligible to receive land, was replaced by 'citizen'. As their status as citizens of Botswana was never in question, the entitlement of Bushmen to land is now unequivocal. It remains the government's task, at both national and local levels, to translate that entitlement into practice.

At the local level, however, it seems that Land Boards pay little heed to the Bushmen's status as citizens. Because culturally ingrained prejudice persists, Tswana applicants for land still tend to be favoured over Basarwa.

Nationally, there are some hopeful signs. In some cases the government has withdrawn land being considered for commercial ranching purposes. In others, it has offered small cash compensations and various compromises, and in each of the blocks of TGLP ranches it has set aside farms and settlements as well as 'communal service centres'.

In Namibia, after independence, the claims for land by some of the country's Bushman citizens have been somewhat more successful. A delegation of Ju/'hoansi attended the 1991 National Conference on Land Reform and the Land Question held in Windhoek, with the aim of securing rights to their ancestral lands in the Nyae Nyae region. The results were favourable, in part because the delegates had a well-prepared case, bringing along maps that charted their traditional n!ores. What also worked in their favour was that for a decade they had been effective in their efforts at community organisation, economic management and 'participatory development', undertaken jointly with a well-funded and well-managed NGO and a local council. While land tenure is not yet securely in Ju/'hoansi hands, the Ju/'hoansi are the only Bushmen in Namibia whose communal title to their ancestral land has been officially recognised.

One or two groups in South Africa have had land claims ruled in their favour. The claimants are the people of Schmidtsdrift and those from the Kalahari Gemsbok National Park (and, by extension, Kagga Kamma, where some of them live and work). The latter, who claim ≠Khomani ancestry, have been allocated a 20 000 hectare stretch of land. It lies adjacent to the national park claimed as their ancestral lands by the ≠Khomani. In early 1996 the !Xu and Khwe Trust entered into negotiations with the government on the purchase of freehold farms near Kimberley, so that those Schmidtsdrift people who wished to stay in the area could live there and raise crops and stock.

The initiatives with the most chance of success for the improvement of their prospects are those that come from the Bushman people themselves, rather than from more or less reluctant, pressured governments.

10.1: *Kalahari, March 1999. Thabo Mbeki embraces David Kruiper, the leader of the ≠Khomani, after the signing of the land restitution agreement while Minister of Land Affairs Derek Hanekom (left) and Northern Cape premier Manie Dipico (right) applaud.*

In Botswana the first process happened dramatically at the 1989 elections, in the Ghanzi district where Bushmen make up almost half the population. By contrast to the previous election campaign in 1984, in 1989 they not only voted in large numbers but fielded seven of the twenty candidates running for District Council office. Three of the Bushman candidates were elected, one of them a woman. She was the most outspoken of the three councillors and very popular with the farm Bushmen. They lamented her death in 1993, and attended her funeral in large numbers. In an animated discussion with four farm Bushmen in Ghanzi in 1997, I was told that people believe her death to have been caused by sorcery, directed against her by her political enemies, specifically blacks who were unable to countenance a Bushman person holding political power and authority.

The death from stomach cancer of John Hardbattle in 1996, the spokesperson of the First People of the Kalahari (see Box 31), was explained in like manner. One of the old men told me that his grown-up son had considered running at the last district election but decided not to, in view of this threat. Yet, he still might, the man said, because he was angry about the condition and treatment of the Bushmen in the district and the land.

Another way for people to vote is 'with their feet': to show their frustration and resolve in the face of a problem issue by walking away from it. The Ju/'hoansi at Tsumkwe, as well as the Ghanzi Bushmen at a number of government settlements, resorted to this measure when the problems in their communities got out of hand and made life unbearable. People simply got up and left, along with their stock animals and their belongings. In Ghanzi this was not much of a solution, however, as there were really no alternative places where life was any better. Some have returned to the farming block, to seek work or to stay with employed relatives, or to D'Kar village attached to the Kuru Development Trust, which, with approximately a thousand residents, is severely overcrowded.

The option available to the Tsumkwe Ju/'hoansi was more favourable: they were able to return to their old band territories, leading quite self-sufficient lives based on foraging, herding and agriculture, as well as some wage labour. Another consideration was political: by returning to their *n!ores* they were able to consolidate their occupancy rights to their ancestral lands. The process started as early as 1982 and became more organised and expanded after the establishment, in 1986, of the Ju/'hoansi's own farmers' union. By October 1987 ten communities had been established in the Nyae Nyae region, with herds of livestock ranging from 15 to 77 head. By 1993 thirty-five groups had returned to their *n!ores*. This process of decentralisation and movement back to the land is similar to the 'outstation' movement of Australian Aborigines a decade earlier, which saw disillusioned and disgruntled foraging people return to their traditional totemic lands, rekindling both traditional culture and a sense of community and political purpose.

Two initiatives with a broader scope have been taken by the Ghanzi Bushmen. One is a Bushman-formed and -run political action group, the Kgeikani Kweni, 'The First People' (of the Kalahari); the other a community organisation and networking group, WIMSA (Working Group of Indigenous Minorities in Southern Africa), which was founded by two expatriate development workers.

Whereas The First People organises and motivates the Bushmen primarily of the Ghanzi district, WIMSA operates at an interregional level that encompasses Bushman communities in all countries of southern Africa.

31 • The First People of the Kalahari •

Kgeikani Kweni has received much attention in local development circles and in the media nationally and internationally. Founded in 1992, and granted legal status as an NGO by the Botswana government the following year, the group's spokesperson was the late John Hardbattle.

10.2: *Logo of Kgeikani Kweni*

European Alliance for Indigenous Populations. Elected representatives from twelve of the RAD settlements from the Ghanzi district and the Central Kalahari Game Reserve make up the Board of Kgeikani Kweni. The organisation informs these communities of their political rights and promotes a positive sense of cultural heritage among the Bushmen. They prefer to call themselves the 'N/oa Khwe, the 'Red – as against black and white – People', or simply Khwe (adding yet another set of terms to the long list of designations for the Bushman people).

A person of mixed descent, Hardbattle was fluent in both Nharo and English. This, coupled with a strong, passionate and articulate concern for Bushman rights, made him an effective spokesman at conferences and meetings abroad where he networked with representatives from other Fourth World minorities. He made presentations at the Human Rights Conference in Geneva in 1994 and at the Working Group on Indigenous Populations at the United Nations in New York.

Other Kgeikani Kweni delegates spoke before the High Commission of the United Nations, the United States Senate, the House of Lords of the United Kingdom and the

Kgeikani Kweni monitors the actions and policies of the government. Cases of mistreatment of farm workers or settlement residents by farmers or game officials are brought to the attention of the law and the media. The group is also mapping the Central Kalahari Game Reserve band territories and water holes, as ammunition in its struggle against government attempts to force its people out of the reserve.

32 • Speaking with one voice, acting for one cause •

The goals of WIMSA are the inter-regional ones of raising the Bushmen's political consciousness and astuteness, and the local ones of generating effective community organisation and leadership at village and grassroots level, along with economic self-sufficiency.

Communities that experience economic or political problems because of government action or inaction receive material and at times legal advice from WIMSA. The group interacts with government in a co-operative rather than an adversarial manner and builds on positive developments.

An especially noteworthy scheme which WIMSA is pursuing with the Cape Town-based South African San Institute (SASI) is the repatriation of Angolan Bushmen from South Africa to reclaim their ancestral lands. Some of these are riddled with landmines. It is planned to provide the Bushmen themselves with the training to carry out the task of de-mining.

Problems

All these promising developments are merely beginnings. Topping the list of problems that delegates brought to the WIMSA conference at Gross Barmen in 1996 was the issue of land security. Others include problems of leadership, poverty, difficulties in gaining access to government, discriminatory and disrespectful behaviour towards Bushmen, and tourism problems. Dealing with these was WIMSA's priority also in its first year of operations in 1996. A year later, at the high-profile Khoesaan Identity and Cultural Heritage conference at Cape Town, attended by about a dozen Khoesaan groups from South Africa, Botswana and

Namibia, similar concerns were voiced by the Bushman delegates. They were from the Kalahari Gemsbok Park, Schmidtsdrift, Nyae Nyae, Ghanzi and Moremi (the game reserve in Botswana from which the Khoe were evicted after its declaration in 1963).

The land issue has cropped up again and again in this account of the Bushmen's present and recent past. While the outlook seems promising for two or three groups in Namibia and South Africa, for others the land issue is still unresolved.

The Kxoe of the western Caprivi, after losing their traditional lands in favour of a game reserve, are still waiting for the land allotments each family was to receive, while those families who have received their agricultural plots of four hectares are uncertain whether these have been registered in their names. Chief Kipi George, the leader of the Kxoe, is actively campaigning on this issue. He has even put their case before the United Nations. One plan is that the Kxoe would use part of the West Caprivi Game Reserve as a conservancy, to manage its resources and its utilisation by tourists and trophy hunters. Their initiative of operating a community-based campsite at Popa Falls was quashed by the Namibian government in 1997, when it evicted the Kxoe from the site. The Kxoe have taken the government to court over the issue.

Another Namibian case of promises and red-tape delays is that of the Hai//om. Here, the level of frustration on the people's part resulted in protest action and police arrests. After years of 'empty promises' regarding the people's request for compensation for the land they had lost through and after the establishment of the Etosha National Park, the Hai//om held a demonstration at the entrance gates of Etosha Park in January 1997 and handed out leaflets to bemused tourists. The police moved in and seventy-three demonstrators were arrested.

Another form of inaction is that governments tolerate land 'invasions' of Bushman settlements, farms or villages by cattle people. The Ghanzi settlement faced the same problem. It is a problem also for the ≠Au//eisi Bushmen in Omaheke district, many of whom are giving way to Herero cattle owners who moved on to some of the half dozen, now badly over-grazed small farms that the Namibian government allocated to the ≠Au//eisi

33 • 'I do not understand this rule where people are trafficked like cattle that are taken to the Botswana Meat Corporation' •

The government of Botswana is determined to get the Khwe 'Bushman' people to leave their ancestral land in the Central Kalahari Game Reserve (CKGR). But the people are resisting and asserting their right to the land.

The Khwe are one of the San or Bushman peoples, who are the original inhabitants of the Kalahari Desert. In the 1960s the 52 000 square kilometre CKGR was set up as a haven for them, as well as the animals they hunted. Until 1997, about 1000 people lived there permanently, while another 2500–3000 had the right according to custom to travel and hunt there. The majority of the inhabitants were Khwe. Though originally hunters and gatherers they had begun to grow a few crops and keep some livestock, and were now settled for much of the time in villages, including the official government settlement at Xade. There were also Kgalagadi, another minority people, living in the south of the reserve.

Since 1986 the Botswana government has had plans to move the Khwe and the Bakgalagadi out of the CKGR. Two reasons are given: that it is necessary to preserve the wildlife and enhance the tourism potential of the reserve; and that the people must be rescued from their allegedly miserable life 'among animals' and moved into settlements, so as to integrate with the rest of Botswana society. The first reason contradicts the government's own conservation and tourism policy, whereby management of game reserves is shared with local communities. The Khwe say their intimate knowledge of the natural resources puts them in a better position than

most to manage the plants and animals, given the chance. As for the second, they do not think they need to be rescued from living in their own country and have shown great resistance to moving, in spite of years of persuasion. As one man said: 'I will not agree to migrate from my ancestral land where my soul and spirits are. I do not understand this rule where people are trafficked like cattle that are taken to the Botswana Meat Corporation.' Previous government settlements, though they may have clinics and schools, provide almost no land or employment and are places of social breakdown and despair.

However, neither of these reasons adequately explains the effort put into moving the people out. Many suspect another reason altogether: the wish to exploit the large diamond deposits suspected to be in the Reserve. Here also plans are being made to lease parts of the reserve for luxury tourism.

In 1996 the government finally announced that the Khwe must move out. This led to world-wide protests, in response to which the government promised that no one would be moved out by force. Nevertheless, in May 1997, they resettled the people from the Xade settlement to 'New Xade' just outside the Reserve. Notwithstanding the government's denials, the residents claim that they were forcibly removed. The site at 'New Xade' has as yet no water supply or permanent buildings, and life there is bleak. It is also in a 'wildlife management area' where the Khwe cannot hold title to the land, and development is restricted.

shortly after independence.

One group has given up trying to succeed in their own community (at Aminus in Corridor 17), and in 1996 accepted a contract with an international tourism game lodge (IntuAfrika) outside the district, to work as guides and as semi-naked, skin-clad human displays in a 'traditional Bushman village'. Two cases of action of the wrong kind were brought to WIMSA's attention. In 1997 a Tswana man dug a well, with the assistance of members of the Kxoe community of Shaikarowe in Ngamiland, and then successfully applied for a land allocation. The people were then removed by trucks from their village to another location. Another group, who had lived for generations near the Tsodilo Hills in Ngamiland and earned income from guiding tourists to the many rock paintings at the site, reported that they had been moved to another village in trucks, making way for Mbukushu people and their cattle. The Mbukushu have also taken over the tourist-guiding job.

A case of repressive action is that of the !Xade (Xade) residents of the Central Kalahari Game Reserve, affecting about a thousand G/wi and //Gana Bushmen. It has received world-wide attention, including that of 'Survival International' who, on 19 March 1998, sent one of their Internet 'Urgent Action Bulletins' to concerned individuals and groups everywhere. Entitled 'Botswana: Last Bushmen in Kalahari Reserve Resist Eviction', the bulletin provides a clear update on this disturbing issue (see Box 33).

Cultural heritage

In addition to the problems of land and political rights, another issue which many of today's Bushmen regard as contentious is the gradual erosion of Bushman culture. This is a problem especially among the younger people, in part because of the education they receive in residential schools in a non-Bushman language, in part because of the power and seductiveness of Western culture, which insinuates its way into that of the Bushmen.

I saw a most poignant expression of this in Ghanzi in 1994 when a disco dance around mega-speakers on a beer-laden truck drowned out a trance dance some of the older people of D'Kar village tried to get going. Many of the disco dancers

were of the younger generation, some of them wearing T-shirts with Western sports or corporate logos. The owner of the truck and sound system was a local black 'entertainment entrepreneur' who helped relieve the Bushman workers of their week's wages.

Tourism, specifically ethno-tourism which has become prevalent all over southern Africa in recent years, is another development likely to undermine the cultural integrity of the Bushmen. This is less of a problem in those community-run, revenue-generating operations that present the Bushmen as they are today, offering camping facilities, accommodation in traditionally built huts, nature walks and crafts for sale. Three such operations have recently been set up. Two are in Namibia: the Omatako Valley Rest Camp and the Makuri camp site, both in the Otjozondjupa region. The other is the Dqãe Qare Camp run by the Kuru Development Trust on a Ghanzi farm which the Dutch government donated in

10.2: *Brochure cover of Bona Safaris.*

10.3: *Kalahari, April 1999: joy at the return of land to the ≠Khomani.*

Botswana. Here tourists see what non-traditional, non-foraging Bushmen do today, such as gardening, stockranching, leather tanning and saddle making, and find out what they want and are working towards. One way this is conveyed is to show the tourists the various development projects run at the D'Kar village by the NGO (the Kuru Development Trust) stationed there. Another operation of this sort is the 'San Cultural Village' which SASI is planning to set up at Cape Point. In addition to being a place for tourists, the village will also be a centre for training interested Bushman people from all over southern Africa in community-based tourism.

International tourists, however, seem to prefer another kind of Bushman: scantily clad, with animal skins over bared skin, toting a bow and arrow or digging stick, a gnu tail and dance rattles, talking dreamily and poetically, ideally in a click language, of the hunter's kinship with animals and the

wind, of arrow poison and love bows, sacred fire and spirits of the veld and of the dead. In such Westerners the Bushmen, as an ancient foraging people, evoke romantic nostalgia and a sense, probably subliminal, of Western cultural superiority. This sort of experience is on offer at a number of places, especially at the two upmarket tourist resorts, Kagga Kamma in South Africa and Intu-Afrika in Namibia. In addition there are some smaller operations run by whites on their farms. For example, Bona Safaris offers three-day tours from Windhoek to Gobabis, the highlight of which is to visit a 'Kung Bushman clan'.

Some Bushman communities have demanded that restrictions be placed on tourists who come uninvited and unencumbered by any government regulations, to photograph people and intrude on their privacy, leaving litter and tainted water (after bathing in the drinking-water reservoirs). At one community, Ka/gae in the Ghanzi district, people make no bones about what they think of tourists: visitors are given a flyer that starts with the words 'You are not welcome here'.

However, it is also possible for tourism to boost cultural integrity and people's sense of identity. It may revitalise culture, as people rediscover or re-emphasise forgotten, ignored or neglected features. In the process, these may also be reconstituted and reinvented, or even invented! The miniature bow and arrow set, which is sold to tourists as a 'love bow', along with fictive explanations as to their use in Bushman courtship, is derived from Western fancies.

Another significant aspect of their lives and their heritage that may be rediscovered and recaptured is their history. The /Uihaba dances performed by Ju/'hoan schoolchildren at 'tribal dance' competitions have become popular in the country; a similar case is the sort of 'tribal dancing' Ghanzi Bushmen may perform at festive occasions, in front of visiting dignitaries. Such dancing is based on the trance curing dance ritual. However, it leaves out the ritual part, fastening instead on the element of hilarity and clowning that frequently precedes these serious moments when trance sets in and *n/om* gets 'hot'. This part is left out of these 'secular' entertainment-geared versions of the trance dance.

Another instance of revitalising and reinventing tradition is the work being done at D'Kar and Schmidtsdrift, by artists who have produced striking paintings and prints.

The Bushmen's struggle for recognition, rights and land, along with the struggles of other South African peoples of Khoesaan ancestry (most prominently the Griqua), received a boost at the 1997 international Khoesaan Identities and Cultural Heritage conference held by the former coloured University of the Western Cape in Cape Town. Coloured people, who have for centuries struggled with the problem of identity, have come to link theirs to the Khoesaan. At this high-profile conference they expressed a common cause with Bushmen all over the region. Namibian and Botswanan delegates had also been invited, and spoke at the event. Strengthened, in numbers, purpose and resolve, with their voices heard loud and clear, the Bushmen see the likelihood of their struggle moving towards a successful outcome in the coming millennium. It remains for governments to listen, to hear and to act.

Survival

In most places around the world, hunting and gathering have given way to other lifestyles. The Bushmen of southern Africa put up a stiff resistance but they were unable to protect their vital resources – game, land and water – from being taken over by crop and pastoral farmers.

By the early 1900s, small groups of Bushmen living in poverty could still be found in what became the Union of South Africa. In time they also disappeared, or lost their identity, and the notion of a 'vanished race' gained ground.

The great quantity of rock art which the San left behind intrigued Europeans. Many saw it as the relic of a people about whom little else was likely to be known. In 1872 a geologist who was working between Prieska and Upington found drawings made by pecking out the stone. He saw 'sandstone, having a flat top, coated black by a thin film of iron oxide. On this are the outlines of two elands, a gemsbok, a hyaena, and two rhinoceroses. A sharp stone has been used to form the lines by repeated blows. The contour of the elands is capital. The Bushmen who make these figures show a great amount of observation, and also the power of drawing with exactness.'

The artist Thomas Baines was less impressed by paintings he was shown, east of the Fish River: 'The works of the aboriginal artists, which covered the face of the cliff to an average height of five feet from the ground, comprised rude but recognisable delineations of the rhinoceros, hartebeeste, giraffe, eland, koodoo, the domestic ox, and other animals, with grotesque representations of men engaged in chase or war, as well as many in which it was impossible to trace a resemblance to any living creature whatever.'

The idea that Bushmen were heading for extinction spurred social scientists and others to study known survivors. Some of these investigators resumed the old debates, such as the relationship between hunters and herders, and new debates about the nature of Bushman culture and other matters began. Belatedly it was recognised that Bushmen, in surprising numbers, had survived –

'against the odds'.

And so – where are the Bushmen today?

This book has to do with the approximately 105 000 Bushmen living in the various countries of southern Africa. Many thousands more, who go by other names, claim a share of Bushman ancestry.

Everyone in southern Africa shares Bushman culture in its various forms. Poets and other writers use the fables and oral histories that were preserved by people like the Bleeks, or that may be heard from living Bushmen today.

Bushman place names have entered common usage, although their origins may not be known. A traveller in the 1800s wrote: 'The Gouph [Koup]! Mysterious word! What means it? ... in the Bushman tongue [it] means vet or fat, a term applied by hunters to a bee's nest filled to the brim with luscious honey; hence not inaptly given ... to that broad belt of country – 100 miles across – between the Zwarteberg and the Nieuwveld ...'

Rock art images are today employed – sometimes insensitively – by advertisers, decorators and designers around the globe.

Bushman rituals, especially those associated with rainmaking, survive in regions from where the Bushmen themselves have long since disappeared. Around Tsolo in the eastern Cape, for example, the anthropologist Frans Prins has found that 'the southern San continue to be relevant, "alive" and influential'.

In recent years Bushmen have begun to return to places where their forebears died, from which they were forced to flee or where they were absorbed by other populations. Members of the Kruiper family of the Kalahari recently lived for a time in the Kagga Kamma private game reserve, in the Cape's Cedarberg, where they displayed 'their age-old skills and traditions' for tourists. A 'Bushman village' is planned for Cape Point where individuals will be trained to operate and profit from the tourist industry. Schemes such as these need care, and the active participation of the Bushmen, to ensure that opportunities – not exploitation – prevail.

34 • Bushman art and artists today •

10.4: *The Kuru artist Thamai Setshogo at work on a lino print, photographed at D'Kar in 1995.*

Under the auspices of the Kuru Development Trust and the !Xu and Khwe Trust, about a dozen men and women in each of these communities were provided with materials and basic training. Other than occasional visits to rock art sites – at Tsodilo Hills, the Brandberg and Magaliesberg – which might provide inspiration and motifs to the artists, they receive no coaching on the subject matter or style of their work. They paint veld scenes, of animals and hunting and of plants and food gathering, the favourite set of motifs of the Kuru male and female artists respectively. The women also like to paint bead-decorated skin bags and skirts, as well as birds and people engaged in group activities, such as visiting and dancing.

Another motif is 'modern' scenes such as trucks, helicopters, houses, cattle, Boer farmers and their wives, watches, jeans, shoes, guitars, radios and other consumer goods.

A third theme, one especially favoured by the late Qwaa, D'Kar's master painter, is the combining of traditional with new motifs, in whimsical, arresting juxtapositions, such as the trickster god //Guwa pointing with an insect-clawed hand at a row of wrist watches, the rounds of their dials reappearing in the stare of the spirit-figure's huge eyes. Another picture blends old and new in a way that, while more subtle artistically, is more explicit politically. We see a pastoral scene of eland grazing and lazing in the grass-green veld. Each bears on its thigh a brand, as do the Ghanzi farmers' cattle, but here of the artist's name.

10.5: *Painting by Coex'ae Bob entitled 'Two women and veld plants'.*

10.6: *Two ratels by Thamai Kaashe.*

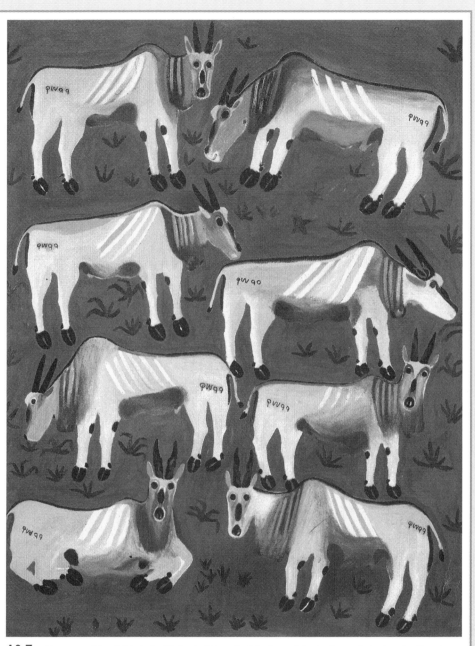

10.7: *Qwaa considered this to be his best picture. In it he lays claim to the ecological and cultural resources of the Bushmen. The artist's work symbolises, perhaps, the struggle of the Bushmen of southern Africa: their demand, on the one hand, for rights in the new economy and polity, and their active steps towards realising them and, on the other, their insistence that this happen in a world that will recognise and tolerate their distinctive identity.*

Sources of Illustrations

Chapter 1

Figure 1.1: Photo: A.B. Smith.
Figure 1.2: Gordon Atlas, Rijksprentenkabinet, Rijksmuseum, Amsterdam.

Chapter 2

Figure 2.1: Poster from IUSPP Congress, Forli, Italy, 1996.
Figure 2.2: H.J. Deacon & J. Deacon, *Human Beginnings in South Africa*, Cape Town, 1999, Figure 5.5.
Figure 2.3: *The Star*, Johannesburg.
Figure 2.4: Deacon & Deacon, *Human Beginnings in South Africa*, Fig. 5.4.
Figure 2.5: MuseumAfrica, Johannesburg.
Figure 2.6: Deacon & Deacon, *Human Beginnings in South Africa*, Fig. 8.23.
Figure 2.7: Deacon & Deacon, *Human Beginnings in South Africa*, Fig. 6.5.

Chapter 3

Figure 3.1: National Botanical Institute, Pretoria, *Flowering Plants of Africa*, no. 1021.
Figure 3.2: National Botanical Institute, Pretoria, *Flowering Plants of Africa*, nos. 745 & 1021.
Figure 3.3: Map: A.B. Smith.
Figure 3.4: Diagram: John Parkington.
Figure 3.5: Gordon Atlas, Rijksprentenkabinet, Rijksmuseum, Amsterdam.
Figure 3.6: D. Lewis-Williams & T. Dowson, *Images of Power*, Johannesburg, 1989, Fig. 56.
Figure 3.7: R. Kuper, *Weise Dame – Röter Riese: Felsbilder aus Namibia*, Cologne, 1991, p. 9.

Figure 3.8: R. Yates, J. Parkington & T. Manhire, *Pictures from the Past*, Pietermaritzburg, 1990, Fig. 29.
Figure 3.9: Photo: A.B. Smith.
Figure 3.10: Photo: D. Halkett.

Chapter 4

Figure 4.1: P. Kolb, *The Present State of the Cape of Good Hope …*, London, 1731. National Library, Cape Division.
Figure 4.2: National Library, Cape Division.
Figure 4.3: National Library, Cape Division.
Figure 4.4: National Library, Cape Division.
Figure 4.5: Map: Chris Berens.
Figure 4.6: Photo: © Sven Ouzman, Rock Art Department, National Museum, South Africa.

Chapter 5

Figure 5.1: Painting by S. Daniell. National Library, Cape Division.
Figure 5.2: National Library, Cape Division.
Figure 5.3: National Library, Cape Division.
Figure 5.4: W.J. Burchell, *Travels in the Interior …*, London, 1822, vol. 1, pp. 162–163.
Figure 5.5: Gordon Atlas, RM32, Rijksprentenkabinet, Rijksmuseum, Amsterdam.

Chapter 6

Figure 6.1: From J.G. Wood, *The Natural History of Man*, vol. 1, London, 1868. National Library, Cape Division.
Figure 6.2: Photo: Stanford Papers, Jagger Library, University of Cape Town.

Figure 6.3:   Bleek Papers, Jagger Library, University of Cape Town, BC151 D2.6.

Figure 6.4: Photographed in the Cape Town studio of W. Hermann in the late 1800s. National Library, Cape Division.

Figure 6.5: National Library, Cape Division, from Library of Parliament: A PIC MEND 36940 (xi).

Figure 6.6: SPCK publication. National Library, Cape Division.

Figure 6.7: *Transactions of the London [Missionary] Society*, vol. 2. National Library, Cape Division.

Figure 6.8: *Die Burger*, 13 February 1971.

Chapter 7

Figure 7.1: Photo: Ethnology Album, National Library, Cape Division.

Figure 7.2: Photo: National Library, Cape Division.

Figure 7.3: Photo: Bushman Folklore Album, National Library, Cape Division.

Figure 7.4: Photo: Bushman Folklore Album, National Library, Cape Division.

Figure 7.5: Photo: Ethnology Album 167, National Library, Cape Division.

Figure 7.6: Photo: Bushman Folklore Album, National Library, Cape Division.

Chapter 8

Figure 8.1: Photo: Mat Guenther.
Figure 8.2: Photo: Hessel Visser.
Figure 8.3: Photo: Mat Guenther.
Figure 8.4: Photo: R.B. Lee.
Figure 8.5: Photo: R.B. Lee.
Figure 8.6: Photo: R.B. Lee.
Figure 8.7: Photo: R. Jacobsen.

Chapter 9

Figure 9.1: Photo: Mat Guenther.
Figure 9.2: Photo: Mat Guenther.
Figure 9.3: Photos: R. Jacobsen.
Figure 9.4: Photo: R.B. Lee.
Figure 9.5: Photo: Mat Guenther.

Chapter 10

Figure 10.1: Photo: Benny Gool (Trace Images).
Figure 10.2: Logo: Kgeikani Kweni.
Figure 10.3: Brochure: Bona Safaris.
Figure 10.4: Photo: Benny Gool (Trace Images).
Figure 10.5: Photo: Mat Guenther.
Figure 10.6: Photo: Mat Guenther.
Figure 10.7: Photo: Mat Guenther.
Figure 10.8: Photo: Mat Guenther.

Bibliography

Chapter 1

Boonzaier, E., Malherbe, C., Smith, A.B. & Berens, P. 1996. *The Cape Herders*. Cape Town: David Philip.

Elphick, R.H. 1974, 1975. The meaning, origin and use of the terms Khoikhoi, San and Khoisan. *Cabo* 2(2):2, 3–7, 12–15.

Schapera, I. & Farrington, E. 1933. *The Early Cape Hottentots*. Van Riebeeck Society.

Smith, A.B. 1998. Khoesaan orthography. *South African Archaeological Bulletin* 53:37–38.

Waterhouse, G. 1932. *Simon van der Stel's Journal of his Expedition to Namaqualand, 1685–6*. Dublin: Hodges, Figgis.

Chapter 2

Blumenschine, R.J. & Cavallo, J.A. 1992. Scavenging and human evolution. *Scientific American* 267 (Oct):70–76.

Clarke, R.J. 1998. First ever discovery of a well-preserved skull and associated skeleton of *Australopithecus*. *South African Journal of Science* 94:460–463.

Deacon, H.J. & Deacon, J. 1999. *Human Beginnings in South Africa*. Cape Town: David Philip.

Henshilwood, C. & Sealy, J. 1997. Bone artefacts from the Middle Stone Age at Blombos Cave, southern Cape, South Africa. *Current Anthropology* 38: 890–895.

Renfrew, C. & Bahn, P. 1991. *Archaeology: Theories, Methods and Practice*. London: Thames and Hudson.

Chapter 3

Archer, F.M. 1994. Ethnobotany of Namaqualand: The Richtersveld. Unpublished M.A. Thesis, University of Cape Town.

Deacon, H.J. 1976. *Where Hunters Gathered*. Claremont: South African Archaeological Society

Deacon, J. 1988. The power of a place in understanding southern San rock engravings. *World Archaeology* 20:129–140.

Dunn, E.J. 1872. Through Bushmanland. *Cape Monthly Magazine* (n.s.) 5(30):374–384.

Hall, S. 1997. Freshwater fish from Mzinyashana Shelter 1, Thukela Basin, KwaZulu-Natal. *Natal Museum Journal of Humanities* 9:47–55.

Jerardino, A. & Parkington, J. 1993. New evidence for whales on archaeological sites in the south-western Cape. *South African Journal of Science* 98:6–7.

Jerardino, A. & Swanepoel, N. 1999. Painted slabs from Steenbokfontein Cave: the oldest known parietal art in Southern Africa. *Current Anthropology* 40:542–548.

Lewis-Williams, D. & Dowson, T. 1989. *Images of Power: Understanding Bushman Rock Art*. Johannesburg: Southern Books.

Mazel, A.D. 1996. Maqonqo Shelter: the excavation of Holocene deposits in the eastern Biggarsberg, Thukela Basin, South Africa. *Natal Museum Journal of Humanities* 8:1–39.

Parkington, J. & Poggenpoel, C. 1971. Excavations at De Hangen, 1968. *South African Archaeological Bulletin* 26:3–36.

Parkington, J., Reeler, C., Nilssen, P. & Henshilwood, C. 1992. Making sense of space at Dunefield midden campsite, western Cape, South Africa. In Smith, A.B. & Mütti, B. (eds.), *Guide to Archaeological Sites in the Southwestern Cape*. Southern African Association of Archaeologists.

Raper, P.E. & Boucher, M. 1988. *Robert Jacob Gordon: Cape Travels, 1777 to 1786*. Johannesburg: Brenthurst.

Sampson, C.G. & Sadr, K. 1999. Khoekhoe ceramics of the upper Seacow River Valley. *South African Archaeological Bulletin* 54:3–15

Sealy, J.C. & Van der Merwe, N.J. 1986. Isotope assessment and the seasonal mobility hypothesis in the south-western Cape, South Africa. *Current Anthropology* 27:135–150.

Smith, A.B. 1993. Exploitation of marine mammals by prehistoric Cape herders. *South African Journal of Science* 89:162–165.

Smith, A.B., Sadr, K., Gribble, J. & Yates, R. 1991. Excavations in the south-western Cape, South Africa, and the archaeological identity of prehistoric hunter-gatherers within the last 2000 years. *South African Archaeological Bulletin* 46:71–91.

Chapter 4

Abrahams, Y. 1994. Resistance, pacification and consciousness: a discussion of the historiography of Khoisan resistance from 1972 to 1993 and Khoisan resistance from 1652 to 1853. Unpublished MA Thesis, Queen's University, Ontario.

Boonzaier, E., Malherbe, C., Smith, A. & Berens, P. 1996. *The Cape Herders*. Cape Town: David Philip.

Burchell, W.J. 1953 (1822–24). *Travels in the Interior of Southern Africa*, 2 vols. London: The Batchworth Press.

Campbell, J. 1974 (1815). *Travels in South Africa*. Cape Town: Struik.

Cullinan, P. 1992. *Robert Jacob Gordon 1743–1795: The Man and his Travels at the Cape*. Cape Town: Struik, Winchester.

Elphick, R. 1985. *Khoikhoi and the Founding of White South Africa*. Johannesburg: Ravan Press.

Forbes, V.S. (ed.) 1975, 1977. Anders Sparrman, *A Voyage to the Cape of Good Hope Towards the Antarctic Polar Circle round the World and to the Country of the Hottentots and the Caffres from the Year 1772–1776*, 2 vols. Cape Town: Van Riebeeck Society.

Hutton, C.W. (ed.) 1964 (1887). *The Autobiography of the Late Sir Andries Stockenström, Bart.*, 2 vols. Cape Town: Struik.

Jolly, P. 1996. Between the lines: some remarks on 'Bushman' ethnicity. In Skotnes, P. (ed.), *Miscast: Negotiating the Presence of the Bushmen*. Cape Town: University of Cape Town Press.

Kicherer, J.J. 1804. Narrative of his mission to the Hottentots, & Boschemen. In *Transactions of the Missionary Society*. London: T. Law.

Lee, R. 1979. *The !Kung San: Men, Women and Work in a Foraging Society*. Cambridge University Press.

Le Vaillant, F. 1790. *Travels from the Cape of Good Hope into the Interior Parts of Africa*, 2 vols. London: William Lane.

Macmillan, W.M. 1968 (1927). *The Cape Colour Question: A Historical Survey*. Cape Town: Balkema.

Moodie, D. (ed.) 1960 (1838–41). *The Record, or A Series of Official Papers Relative to the Condition and Treatment of the Native Tribes of South Africa*. Cape Town: Balkema.

Newton-King, S. 1985. The labour market of the Cape Colony, 1807–28. In Marks, S. & Atmore, A. (eds.), *Economy and Society in Pre-industrial South Africa*. London: Longman.

Penn, N. 1995. The Orange River frontier zone, c. 1700–1805. In Smith, A.B. (ed.), *Einiqualand: Studies of the Orange River Frontier*. Cape Town: UCT Press.

—— 1996. 'Fated to perish': the destruction of the Cape San. In Skotnes, P. (ed.), *Miscast: Negotiating the Presence of the Bushmen*. Cape Town: University of Cape Town Press.

Philip, J. 1828. *Researches in South Africa*, 2 vols. London: James Duncan.

Pringle, T. 1966 (1835). *Narrative of a Residence in South Africa*. Cape Town: Struik.

Raidt, E.H. et al. (ed.) 1971, 1973. François Valentyn, *Description of the Cape of Good Hope with the Matters Concerning It*, 2 vols. Cape Town: Van Riebeeck Society.

Raven-Hart, R. (ed.) 1967. *Before Van Riebeeck: Callers at South Africa from 1488 to 1652*. Cape Town: Struik.

Ross, R. 1993. Donald Moodie and the origins of South African historiography. *Beyond the Pale: Essays on the History of Colonial South Africa*. Hanover & London: Wesleyan University Press.

Sahlins, M. 1974. *Stone Age Economics*. London: Tavistock.

Shaw, B. 1970 (1820). *Memorials of South Africa*. Cape Town: Struik.

Stow, G.W. 1964 (1905). *The Native Races of South Africa*. Cape Town: Struik.

Theal, G.M. (ed.) 1897–1905. *Records of the Cape Colony*, 36 vols. London: William Clowes.

Thom, H.B. (ed.) 1952. *Journal of Jan van Riebeeck*, 3 vols. Cape Town & Amsterdam: Balkema.

Chapter 5

Burchell, W.J. 1953. (1822–24). *Travels in the Interior of Southern Africa*, 2 vols. London: The Batchworth Press.

Chidester, D. 1996. Bushman religion: open, closed, and new frontiers. In Skotnes, P. (ed.), *Miscast: Negotiating the Presence of the Bushmen*. Cape Town: University of Cape Town Press.

Cullinan, P. 1992. *Robert Jacob Gordon 1743–1795: The Man and his Travels at the Cape*: Cape Town: Struik, Winchester.

Hutton, C.W. (ed.). 1964 (1880). *The Autobiography of the Late Sir Andries Stockenström, Bart.*, 2 vols. Cape Town: Struik.

Kicherer, J.J. 1804. Narrative of his mission to the Hottentots, & Boschemen. In *Transactions of the Missionary Society*. London: T. Law.

Lichtenstein, H. 1928–30. *Travels in Southern Africa, in the Years 1803, 1804, 1805 and 1806*, 2 vols. Cape Town: Van Riebeeck Society.

Mandelbrote, H.J. (ed.) 1944. O.F. Mentzel, *A Geographical and Topographical Description of the Cape of Good Hope*. Cape Town: Van Riebeeck Society.

Moodie, D. (ed.), 1960 (1838–41). *The Record*. Cape Town: Balkema.

Penn, N. 1996. 'Fated to perish.' In Skotnes, P. (ed.), *Miscast: Negotiating the Presence of the Bushmen*. Cape Town: University of Cape Town Press.

Raven-Hart, R. (ed.), 1971. *Cape Good Hope 1652–1702: The First Fifty Years of Dutch Colonisation as Seen by Callers*, 2 vols. Cape Town: Balkema.

Stow, G.W. 1964 (1905). *The Native Races of South Africa*. Cape Town: Struik.

Thom, H.B. (ed.) 1952. *Journal of Jan van Riebeeck*, 3 vols. Cape Town: Balkema.

Wright, J.B. 1971. *Bushman Raiders of the Drakensberg, 1840–1870*. Pietermaritzburg: University of Natal Press.

Chapter 6

Bradlow, E. & Bradlow, F. (eds.) 1979. *William Somerville's Narrative of His Journeys to the Eastern Cape Frontier and to Lattakoe, 1799–1802*. Cape Town: Van Riebeeck Society.

Campbell, J. 1974 (1815). *Travels in South Africa*. Cape Town: Struik.

Forbes, V.S. (ed.) 1967, 1968. George Thompson, *Travels and Adventures in Southern Africa*, 2 vols. Cape Town: Van Riebeeck Society.

—— 1975, 1977. Anders Sparrman, *A Voyage to the Cape of Good Hope*, 2 vols. Cape Town: Van Riebeeck Society.

—— et al. (eds.) 1986. Carl Peter Thunberg, *Travels at the Cape of Good Hope 1772–1775*. Cape Town: Van Riebeeck Society.

Glenn, I. 1996. The Bushman in early South African literature. In Skotnes, P. (ed.), *Miscast: Negotiating the Presence of the Bushmen*. Cape Town: University of Cape Town Press.

Hutton, C.W. (ed.) 1964 (1887). *The Autobiography of the Late Sir Andries Stockenström, Bart.*, 2 vols. Cape Town: Struik.

Kennedy, R.F. (ed.) 1961, 1964. Thomas Baines, *Journal of Residence in Africa, 1842–1853*, 2 vols. Cape Town: Van Riebeeck Society.

Lye, W.F. (ed.) 1975. *Andrew Smith's Journal of His Expedition into the Interior of South Africa, 1834–36*. Cape Town: Balkema.

Macquarrie, J.W. (ed.) 1958. *The Reminiscences of Sir Walter Stanford*. Cape Town: Van Riebeeck Society.

Malherbe, V.C. 1997. The Cape Khoisan in the Eastern Districts of the Colony before and after Ordinance 50 of 1828. Unpublished Ph.D. Thesis, University of Cape Town.

Marais, J.S. 1968 (1939). *The Cape Coloured People 1652–1937*. Johannesburg: Witwatersrand University Press.

Moodie, D. (ed.) 1960 (1834–41). *The Record*. Cape Town: Balkema.

Pringle, T. 1966 (1835). *Narrative of a Residence in South Africa*. Cape Town: Struik.

Ross, R. 1981. Andries Waterboer. In Beyers, C.J. (ed.), *Dictionary of South African Biography*, IV.

Saunders, C. 1977. Madolo: a Bushman life. *African Studies* 36(2), 145–54.

Wright, J.B. 1971. *Bushman Raiders of the Drakensberg, 1840–1870*. Pietermaritzburg: University of Natal Press.

Chapter 7

Anthing, L. 1863. Report. In Skotnes, P. (ed.), *Miscast: Negotiating the Presence of the Bushmen*. Cape Town: University of Cape Town Press.

Bradlow, E. & Bradlow, F. (eds.) 1979. *William Somerville's Narrative of His Journeys to the Eastern Cape Frontier and to Lattakoe*. Cape Town: Van Riebeeck Society.

Deacon, J. 1996. A tale of two families: Wilhelm Bleek, Lucy Lloyd and the /Xam San of the northern Cape. In Skotnes, P. (ed.), *Miscast: Negotiating the Presence of the Bushmen*. Cape Town: University of Cape Town Press.

—— & Thomas A. Dowson (eds.) 1996. *Voices from the Past: /Xam Bushmen and the Bleek and Lloyd Collection*. Johannesburg: Witwatersrand University Press.

Fouché, L. (ed.) 1932. *Louis Trigardt's Trek across the Drakensberg, 1837–1838*. Cape Town: Van Riebeeck Society.

Kennedy, R.F. (ed.) 1961, 1964. Thomas Baines, *Journal of Residence in South Africa, 1842–1853*, 2 vols. Cape Town: Van Riebeeck Society.

Lye, W.F. (ed.) 1975. *Andrew Smith's Journal of His Expedition into the Interior of South Africa, 1834–36*. Cape Town: Balkema.

Malherbe, V.C. The Cape Khoisan in the Eastern Districts of the Colony before and after Ordinance 50 of 1828. Unpublished Ph.D. Thesis, University of Cape Town.

—— 1985. Khoikhoi and the question of convict transportation from the Cape Colony, 1820–1842. *South African Historical Journal* 17:19–39.

Penn, N. 1996. 'Fated to perish'. In Skotnes, P. (ed.), *Miscast: Negotiating the Presence of the Bushmen*. Cape Town: University of Cape Town Press.

Pringle, T. 1966 (1835). *Narrative of a Residence in South Africa*. Cape Town: Struik.

Ross, R. 1996. The self-image of Jacob Adams. In Skotnes, P. (ed.), *Miscast: Negotiating the Presence of the Bushmen*. Cape Town: University of Cape Town Press.

Wright, J.B. 1971. *Bushman Raiders of the Drakensburg, 1840–1870*. Pietermaritzburg: University of Natal Press.

Chapter 8

Barnard, A. 1992. *Hunters and Herders of Southern Africa*. Cambridge University Press.

Biesele, M. 1993. *Women Like Meat: The Folklore and Foraging Ideology of the Kalahari Ju/'hoansi*. Johannesburg: Witwatersrand University Press.

Guenther, M. 1999. *Tricksters and Trancers: Bushman Religion and Society*. Bloomington: Indiana University Press.

Kent, S. 1992. The current forager controversy: real vs. ideal views of hunter-gatherers. *Man* 27:43–70.

Lee, R.B. 1979. *The !Kung San: Men, Women and Work in a Foraging Society*. Cambridge University Press.

—— 1993. *The Dobe Ju/'hoansi*, 2nd edn. Fort Worth: Harcourt Brace.

—— & Guenther, M. 1993. Problems in Kalahari ethnography and the tolerance of error. *History in Africa* 20:185–235.

Marshall, L. 1976. Sharing, talking and giving: relief of social tension among the !Kung. In Lee, R.B. & DeVore, I. (eds.), *Kalahari Hunter-Gatherers*. Cambridge, Mass.: Harvard University Press.

Schapera, I. 1930. *The Khoisan Peoples of South Africa*. London: Routledge.

Silberbauer, G. 1981. *Hunter and Habitat in the Central Kalahari Desert*. Cambridge University Press.

Solway, J. & Lee, R.B. 1990. Foragers, genuine or spurious? Situating the Kalahari San in history. *Current Anthropology* 31:109–146.

Tobias, P. (ed.) 1978. *The Bushmen*. Cape Town: Human & Rousseau.

Wiessner, P. 1982. Risks, reciprocity and social influences on !Kung San economics. In Leacock, E. & Lee, R.B. (eds.), *Politics and History in Band Societies*. Cambridge University. Press.

Wilmsen, E. & Denbow, J. 1990. Paradigmatic history of San-speaking peoples and attempts at revision. *Current Anthropology* 31:489–524.

Chapter 9

Gordon, R. 1992. *The Bushman Myth: The Making of a Namibian Underclass.* Boulder: Westview Press.

Guenther, M. 1986. *The Nharo Bushmen of Botswana: Tradition and Change.* Hamburg: Helmut Buske Verlag.

Hitchcock, R.K. & Holm, J. 1985. Political development among the Basarwa of Botswana. *Cultural Survival Quarterly* 9:7–11.

—— & Holm, J. 1993. Bureaucratic domination of hunter-gatherer societies: a study of the San of Botswana. *Development and Change* 24:305–338.

Hurlich, S. & Lee, R.B. 1979. Colonialism, apartheid and liberation: a Namibian example. In Turner, D. & Smith, G. (eds.), *Challenging Anthropology.* Toronto: McGraw Hill Ryerson.

Russell, M. & Russell, M. 1979. *Afrikaners of the Kalahari: White Minority in a Black State.* Cambridge University Press.

Sharp, J. & Douglas, S. 1996. Prisoners of their reputation? The veterans of the 'Bushman' battalions in South Africa. In Skotnes, P. (ed.), *Miscast: Negotiating the Presence of the Bushmen.* Cape Town: University of Cape Town Press.

Silberbauer, G. & Kuper, A. 1966. Kgalagadi masters and Bushman serfs: some observations. *African Studies* 25:171–179.

Steyn, H.P. 1994. Role and position of elderly !Xu in the Schmidtsdrift Bushman community. *South African Journal of Ethnology* 17:31–37.

Volkman, T. 1982. *The San in Transition. Vol. 1: A Guide to N!ai, the Story of a !Kung Woman.* Boston: Cultural Survival.

Vorster, L.P. 1995. The !Xu of Schmidtsdrift and sorcery. In Saunders, A.J.G.M. (ed.), *Speaking for the Bushmen.* Gaborone: The Botswana Society.

Wilmsen, E. 1989. *Land Filled with Flies.* Chicago University Press.

Chapter 10

Bank, A. (ed.) 1997. *The Proceedings of the Khoisan Identities and Cultural Heritage Conference.* Cape Town: Institute for Historical Research, University of the Western Cape.

Biesele, M. 1993. Land, language and leadership. Ju/'hoan Bushmen present a model of self-determination, both before and since Namibian independence. *Cultural Survival Quarterly* 17:57–60.

Biesele, M. 1995. Human rights and democratization in Namibia: some grassroots political perspectives. *African Rural and Urban Development* 1(2):49–72.

Buntman, B. 1996. Bushman images in South African tourist advertising: the case of Kagga Kamma. In Skotnes, P. (ed.), *Miscast: Negotiating the Presence of the Bushmen.* Cape Town: University of Cape Town Press.

Hitchcock, R.K. 1996. *Bushmen and the Politics of the Environment in Southern Africa.* IWGIA Document 79. Copenhagen: International Work Group for Indigenous Affairs.

Hitchcock, R.K. & Brandenburgh, R. 1990. Tourism, conservation and culture in the Kalahari Desert, Botswana. *Cultural Survival Quarterly* 14:20–24.

Katz, R., Biesele, M. & St. Denis, V. 1997. *Healing Makes Our Hearts Happy.* Rochester, Vermont: Inner Traditions.

Moeletsi, B. 1993. The Tribal Land Act of Botswana: does it have a place for the Basarwa? In Saugstad, S. & Tsonope, J. (eds.), *Developing Basarwa Research, and Research for Basarwa Development.* Gaborone: National Institute of Development Research and Documentation.

White, H. 1995. *In the Tradition of the Forefathers: Bushman Traditionality at Kagga Kamma.* Cape Town: University of Cape Town Press.

Index

Figures in italics refer to illustrations only.